ISAIAH 56–66

Grace I Emmerson

ISAIAH 56–66

Grace I. Emmerson

To my husband, Peter
and
my brother, Galen

cor ad cor loquitur

Copyright © 1992 Sheffield Academic Press

Published by JSOT Press
JSOT Press is an imprint of
Sheffield Academic Press Ltd
343 Fulwood Road
Sheffield S10 3BP
England

Typeset by Sheffield Academic Press
and
Printed on acid-free paper in Great Britain
The Charlesworth Group, Huddersfield

British Library Cataloguing in Publication Data

Emmerson, Grace I.
    Isaiah 56–66.- (Old Testament Guides
    Series, ISSN 0264-6498)
    I. Title II. Series
    224

ISBN 1-85075-382-2

CONTENTS

PREFACE

I am grateful to the editor for so generously allocating a separate volume to these last chapters of Isaiah. Too often they are given scant attention in comparison with the rest of the book. The importance of the message, the balance and artistry of the structure, and the impressive quality of the poetic imagery make the study of Third Isaiah a rewarding experience.

The use of the expression 'Third Isaiah' does not prejudge the question of single or multiple authorship which is discussed in Chapter 4, but is merely a convenient way of referring to chs. 56–66. Quotations are from the RSV unless otherwise indicated. Chapter and verse numbers are those of the English Version. Where the Masoretic text differs in this respect this is indicated in brackets.

Grace I. Emmerson
University of Birmingham
December 1991

ABBREVIATIONS

AB	Anchor Bible
BETL	Bibliotheca ephemeridum theologicarum lovaniensium
BWANT	Beiträge zur Wissenschaft vom Alten und Neuen Testament
BZAW	Beihefte zur *ZAW*
Ebib	Etudes bibliques
ExpTim	*Expository Times*
HKAT	Handkommentar zum Alten Testament
JBL	*The Journal of Biblical Literature*
JQR	*Jewish Quarterly Review*
JSOT	*Journal for the Study of the Old Testament*
NCB	New Century Bible
NEB	The New English Bible
OTL	Old Testament Library
REB	The Revised English Bible
RSV	The Revised Standard Bible
TLZ	*Theologische Literaturzeitung*
VT	*Vetus Testamentum*
VTSup	*Vetus Testamentum*, Supplements
WBC	Word Biblical Commentary
ZAW	*Zeitschrift für die Alttestamentliche Wissenschaft*
ZTK	*Zeitschrift für Theologie und Kirche*

Select List of Commentaries

Commentaries in English:

J.L. McKenzie, *Second Isaiah* (AB; New York: Doubleday, 1968), useful especially for its introduction; the textual comments are brief.

J. Muilenburg, *Isaiah Chapters 40–66* (Interpreter's Bible, 5; Nashville: Abingdon Press, 1956), particularly helpful on questions of literary form and poetic structure.

C. Westermann, *Isaiah 40–66* (OTL; London: SCM Press/ Philadelphia: Westminster Press, 1969), contains detailed discussion of form criticism.

R.N. Whybray, *Isaiah 40–66* (NCB; London: Oliphants, 1975/Grand Rapids: Eerdmans, 1981), valuable for its detailed comments on text and interpretation, and on relation to Second Isaiah.

Also of interest:

J.D.W. Watts, *Isaiah 34–66* (WBC, 25; Waco, TX: Word Books, 1987), who regards the book of Isaiah as a drama in twelve acts dating in its final form from the fifth century BC.

Among useful short commentaries are:

E. Achtemeier, *The Community and Message of Isaiah 56–66* (Minneapolis: Augsburg, 1982), who considers that these chapters originated among the marginalized in society after the exile.

A.S. Herbert, *Isaiah 40–66* (Cambridge Bible Commentary on the New English Bible; Cambridge: Cambridge University Press, 1975), particularly helpful for the religious significance of the texts.

D.R. Jones, *Isaiah 56–66 and Joel* (Torch Bible Commentaries; London: SCM Press, 1964), stressing the continuity of the Isaiah tradition.

G.A.F. Knight, *The New Israel: A Commentary on the Book of Isaiah 56–66* (International Theological Commentary; Grand Rapids:

Eerdmans, 1985), who understands these chapters as opposition to the priestly group who had returned from exile.

J.F.A. Sawyer, *Isaiah*, II (The Daily Study Bible, Old Testament; Edinburgh: Saint Andrew Press, 1986), a stimulating work for the general reader, with the emphasis on reading the book of Isaiah as a whole.

J. Skinner, *The Book of the Prophet Isaiah Chapters XL-LXVI* (Cambridge Bible; Cambridge: Cambridge University Press, 1917), an older commentary but still useful.

The following stand apart from the mainstream in rejecting the idea of a Third Isaiah and argue for the unity of chs. 40–66:

C.C. Torrey, *The Second Isaiah. A New Interpretation* (Edinburgh: T. & T. Clark, 1928).

J.D. Smart, *History and Theology in Second Isaiah. A Commentary on Is. 35; 40–66* (Philadelphia: Westminster Press, 1965/London: Epworth Press, 1967).

A valuable discussion of English-language commentaries on Isaiah is to be found in R.J. Coggins, 'Which is the Best Commentary? 12. Isaiah', *ExpTim* 102 (1991), pp. 99-102.

Foreign-language commentaries:

P.-E. Bonnard, *Le Second Isaïe, son disciple et leurs éditeurs.* (Ebib; Paris: Gabalda, 1972).

B. Duhm, *Das Buch Jesaia* (HKAT; Gottingen: Vandenhoeck & Ruprecht, 5th edn, 1968) a reprint of the 4th edition, 1922, first published in 1892.

W. Kessler, *Gott geht es um das Ganze. Jesaja lvi-lxvi und xxiv-xxvii* (Die Botschaft des Alten Testaments; Stuttgart, 2nd edn, 1967).

P. Volz, *Jesaja II* (Kommentar zum Alten Testament; Leipzig: Werner Scholl, 1932; repr. Hildesheim: Georg Olms, 1974).

1

INTRODUCTION

IN STUDYING THE PROPHETIC BOOKS of the Old Testament it is a difficult if not impossible task, and by no means the most important, to try to recover the actual words, the *ipsissima verba*, of the prophet. It is widely recognized by scholars that in almost every case the nucleus of the message, which by tradition is ascribed to a particular prophet, has been expanded by the addition of later material. This is not, indeed, a cause for regret but rather an indication of the force and liveliness of the original message which has led to its reapplication to later circumstances and its reinterpretation to meet different and changing needs. It is a recognition that the power of the message was such that its meaning was not exhausted when the situation to which it had originally been addressed had passed. Consequently there has been a growing awareness in recent years of the importance of reading a prophetic book as a whole (see in particular Childs). The meaning of the book as a whole is likely to have a somewhat different perspective from the message in its original context, even if it were possible for us to recover the latter with any certainty. Later layers of tradition must not be ignored. What is chronologically secondary is not, on that account, to be regarded as less important, for it has its own distinctive contribution to make. The process of 'unravelling' is not always possible, nor is it generally of primary importance. The analytical approach which divides material into its constituent parts must always be supplemented by attention to the overall perspective and the significance of the whole. Nowhere is this more evident than in studying the book of Isaiah which is itself the final product of a long and complex process of transmission.

It has for some considerable time been customary in academic circles to divide the 66 chapters of Isaiah into three sections, designated for convenience as First, Second and Third Isaiah. The general distinction in historical background between chs. 1–39 and 40–66 was first detected as long ago as the thirteenth century by the Jewish scholar Ibn Ezra, but it was not until Duhm's epoch-making work in 1892 that it was widely accepted that chs. 40–66 are not themselves a unity. The unmistakably Palestinian background of 56–66 led Duhm to distinguish these chapters from the message of the great exilic prophet to whom 40–55 are attributed, and to identify them as Trito-Isaiah. The history of the Isaianic corpus is, however, far more complex than this simple threefold division might suggest. Although chs. 40–55 are a rare exception among the prophetic books in that they show little evidence of the presence of secondary material (Whybray), the same cannot be said of the other two sections of the book. Behind chs. 1–39 in their present shape lies an immensely complicated process of development. Nevertheless it is possible to see at the heart of these chapters, as is true also of the other eighth-century prophets Amos, Hosea and Micah, a nucleus of material which may safely be attributed to an identifiable prophet located in a specific period of history of which a considerable amount is known. The situation is otherwise when we come to chs. 56–66. Here we face a different set of problems. Unlike many (though not all) of the other prophetic books, there are no historical indicators here to enable us to date with any measure of precision even separate sections of the material, let alone the whole. In fact, the nature of the material is such that the question arises whether it is justifiable at all to think in terms of a single prophet whose work forms the nucleus of these chapters, or whether it is more appropriate to regard 56–66 as a collection of disparate material of uncertain origin.

The insoluble problems presented by these last chapters of Isaiah, the uncertainty as to their authorship and date, and their bewilderingly diverse content, have undoubtedly contributed, in part at least, to the neglect which they have frequently suffered in comparison with the profound attention paid to the rest of the book of Isaiah. They have sometimes been regarded as little more than an appendix, compiled from rather random material, to the messages of two earlier and greater prophets. Yet the high regard in which these words were held in postexilic Judah is evident from the fact that they were cherished and preserved through many vicissitudes of history, and over many generations, to become part of the Jewish and Christian Scriptures. Indeed, the New Testament writers found in them a rich source of prophetic material. Of the numerous quotations or allusions to the book of Isaiah which are to be found in the New Testament, more than one hundred relate to chs. 56–66. The following may serve as a few particularly notable examples: 61.1-2 furnishes the key to Jesus' understanding of his own role (Lk. 4.18-19); the motivation for the cleansing of the temple (Mk. 11.17) comes from 56.7; the description of God's armour in 59.17 is echoed in the Christian's equipment for spiritual warfare (Eph. 6.14-17); and the scene of final judgment in Rev. 19.13-15 draws on the portrayal of the divine warrior in 63.3-6. For our part we need to guard against the tendency of 'setting up the concept of "greatness" as a theological norm and measuring the later prophets by it' (von Rad). The only appropriate question is whether the postexilic prophets genuinely confronted their contemporaries with the challenge of God's message, or whether they failed in that task.

Generally speaking, apart from a very few obscure verses, Third Isaiah is largely free from textual problems. It is the uncertainty of historical background and the consequent difficulty in determining the exact nature of the issues involved and the concerns of the rival factions within the community which present the most serious problems of interpretation.

Further Reading

Details of books mentioned above:

B.S. Childs, *Introduction to the Old Testament as Scripture* (London: SCM Press, 1979).

G. von Rad, *Old Testament Theology*, II (Edinburgh: Oliver & Boyd, 1962).

R.N. Whybray, *The Second Isaiah* (Old Testament Guides; Sheffield: JSOT Press, 1983).

2

STRUCTURE, LITERARY FORM AND POETIC IMAGERY

Haphazard Collection or Sophisticated Arrangement?

AFTER THE POWERFUL CHAPTERS of Second Isaiah with their unified message that Yahweh is not only willing but able to save, chs. 56–66 are likely to seem, at first sight, a bewildering medley of denunciation and promise, warning and hope, lament and confidence. The reader can be forgiven for gaining this impression, for immediately in ch. 56 we are confronted with just such an abrupt transition.

The chapter begins on an optimistic note: the era of salvation is at hand, and this expectation challenges the community to practise justice and engage in righteous action and to eschew evil. Among the general terms used to describe the obligations which God's imminent intervention in salvation demands of his people only one specific requirement is laid down: that of keeping the sabbath (v. 2), a stipulation emphasized twice more in the following verses. Then, as if to underline the newness of the era of salvation, the old restrictive prescription of Deut. 23.1-3 is replaced by a new prophetic *torah* by which both foreigners and eunuchs (the latter concern a hint perhaps of an adjustment to the situation of some who had recently returned home from courtly service in Babylon and Persia) are welcomed into the worshipping community provided that they 'hold fast the covenant' (vv. 4, 6), and in particular its outward and visible expression in observance of the sabbath.

Up to this point in the chapter, then, there is a clear sequence of thought, even though the difference in subject matter between vv. 1-2 and 3-8 suggests that the connection is editorial. The new age of salvation which is at hand is to be marked by the removal of traditional restrictions on access to the temple. Hereafter it will be known as 'a house of prayer for all peoples' (v. 7), for God's concern transcends racial boundaries. Not only will he restore Israel's exiles; he will 'gather yet others to him besides those already gathered' (v. 8). In its present context this is undoubtedly a reference to Gentiles (contrast 11.12). Henceforward, then, membership of the worshipping community is not to be a matter of privilege by virtue of birth and race, but is to be dependent on individual choice—on personal adherence to the covenant, expressed in part by sabbath-keeping. Suddenly, however, the logical sequence is interrupted and the tone changes abruptly to denunciation of the community's leaders (vv. 9-12). The language is searing, and its powerful imagery and moral challenge are in no way inferior to the judgment oracles of pre-exilic prophecy. It is possible to argue that this passage is itself of pre-exilic origin but now applied to new circumstances (so Westermann). Another similarly abrupt transition, this time from denunciation to promise of salvation, occurs in ch. 57, where there seems to be little continuity between the condemnation of idolatry in vv. 3-13 and the assurance offered to the humble and contrite in vv. 14-19.

Yet this first impression that Third Isaiah lacks systematic arrangement is misleading. It is possible to detect, in many instances, the rationale behind the arrangement of the material. As in other prophetic books, there are several examples of the use of catchwords to provide links between originally independent literary units. The following may be given as examples. The similarity of expression between 56.5 ('an everlasting name which shall not be cut off') and 55.13 ('an everlasting sign which shall not be cut off') probably accounts, in part at least, for the placing of what is probably one of the latest parts of Third Isaiah in immediate conjunction with the oracles of Second Isaiah (Jones). Similarly the presence of the catchword *rūaḥ* ('wind' in 59.19, 'spirit' in 59.21) may explain

the present rather awkward position of 59.21, whose prose
style and deuteronomistic flavour strongly suggest that it is
secondary in this context (though on this see further p. 74).
One of the most fascinating examples of the operation of the
catchword principle occurs, in all probability, in ch. 58, where
it is surprising to find such a radical reinterpretation of what
fasting means (vv. 1-12) alongside a thoroughly traditional
attitude towards the sabbath (vv. 13-14). Despite Muilenburg's
argument that vv. 13-14 are integrally related to their context
on the grounds that 'without them the poem remains a torso',
the marked difference in the attitudes adopted towards the
institutions of fasting and sabbath observance seems com-
pelling evidence that their juxtaposition is due to editorial
activity. Moreover, despite certain expressions they have in
common ('seeking your pleasure' vv. 3 and 13; 'my ways' v. 2,
'your ways' v. 13), and the general resemblance of the literary
form of vv. 13-14 to vv. 9b-11 as a conditional promise of
salvation, the exhortation to sabbath-keeping at the end of ch.
58 is closer to 56.1-8, suggesting to Westermann that these
two passages may once have formed a framework to chs. 56–
58 which at one time existed as a separate and independent
unit. It is, therefore, a conjecture worth considering that the
key to the present position of 58.13-14 lies in the resemblance,
unfortunately not apparent in English translation, between
the final word of 58.12, 'to dwell in' (*lašābet*), which in an
unvocalized text could be read as 'for the sabbath' (*laššabbat*),
and the expression 'from the sabbath' (*miššabbat*) in v. 13
(Whybray).

The editorial arrangement of the material in general, however, is more meaningful than a purely mechanical use of
catchwords might suggest. A logical sequence can for the most
part be traced in the arrangement of what were originally
independent units. To put it briefly, the situation described in
57.1 is to be seen as the consequence of the failure of leadership
in 56.10-12 (the verb *bīn* 'to discern' or 'understand' in 56.11 is
echoed in 57.1). The theme of wickedness in 57.20-21 continues in 58.1, 4. 59.1 forms an appropriate sequel to the promise
of ch. 58, reinforcing its conditionality by affirming that when
disaster occurs it is due not to Yahweh's inadequacy but to his

people's sin (here the verb *kbd* is not so much a catchword as a play on two different meanings of the root: 'to honour' in 58.13, 'to be dull, heavy' in 59.1). In 59.14-15 the lament culminates in the assertion that justice, righteousness and truth are lacking in society; in response the divine warrior intervenes precisely because there is no justice (v. 15b). The result of this divine intervention in salvation is the confident summons addressed to Zion to rise from her humiliation, with its attendant promises in 60–62. These in turn are underwritten by the subsequent portrayal of the divine warrior who effects his people's deliverance (63.1-6).

Although at first sight the second portrayal of this warrior figure seems to sit strangely alongside the promises of 60–62, it has important consequences. The vivid description of God's intervention not only reinforces the promises, expanding in dramatic fashion the meaning of the proclamation, 'Behold, your salvation comes' (62.11), but also gives to this impersonal expression a personal content: 'It is I...mighty to save' (63.1). This statement then makes a fitting transition to the praise of Yahweh (63.1-6) which forms the prelude to the lament of 63.7–64.12. Subsequently ch. 65, with its affirmation of Yahweh's patient availability even in the absence of any human response, provides in its present (though not original) context an answer to the final poignant questions with which 64.12 laments the silence of God. Finally, the expression 'my holy mountain' in 65.25, although probably signifying here the land of Israel, is used elsewhere frequently as a designation of Mount Zion, and so provides a link with 66.1 which is concerned with the true nature of God's dwelling-place.

There is yet another feature of these chapters which precludes the view that their present arrangement is the result of anything other than careful and deliberate planning, indeed of artistry, on the part of those responsible for their final form. Far from being a haphazard, unsystematic collection of oracles, these chapters show a remarkable symmetry in their overall structure which cannot be accidental. The pivot is the central section, chs. 60–62, around which the rest of the material is arranged in a series of concentric circles. These three central chapters stand out as distinct from their context in that they comprise unqualified promises of salvation to the entire community. They contain neither denunciation of Israel's sin nor summons to repentance. It is in these central chapters that we find the closest and most frequent reminiscences of Second Isaiah. Surrounding this nucleus are two 'divine warrior' passages (59.15b-20; 63.1-6). Although they differ significantly from each other in many respects (see p. 31), both describe Yahweh's active intervention on behalf of his people, emphasizing especially his initiative as sole saviour: 'I looked, but there was no one to help...so my own arm brought me victory' (63.5; cf. 59.16). Surrounding these are two long liturgical passages (59.1-15a; 63.7–64.12) in which the worshipping community itself, or an appointed spokesman on its behalf, laments the sins which have led to the community's present pitiful plight, a setting which Westermann regards as not merely editorial but indicative of an intrinsic connection which existed between the prophetic message of hope and the services of lamentation held by the community in exile.

Although the content and language of the two laments differ considerably, the symmetry of arrangement is preserved here also in that the first begins and the second ends on the same note, the silence of God (59.1; 64.12). The first of the two laments, by its affirmation that it is not God's inability to hear and save but his people's sin which has disrupted communication between the human and the divine (59.1-2), balances, and in effect answers, the despairing question with which the second lament concludes (64.12). There is symmetry, too, in the arrangement of chs. 57–58 and 65 which precede and follow the two laments. Both condemn idolatrous practices (57.1-13; 65.1-16), and both serve to reassure the faithful (57.14-19 and 58.8-14; 65.8-25). There is no suggestion here, of course, that they originated in similar circumstances, for there is an evident difference in their historical situations: whereas the tension between two rival religious factions permeates 65.8-15, this dichotomy appears only at the beginning and end of ch. 57, creating the strong impression that this element is not integral to the passage but belongs to a later stage in the process of development. Finally, parallels of a rather general kind can be detected in chs. 56 and 66: both are concerned, in different ways, with matters relating to the temple and the offering of sacrifice, and both show a remarkably open attitude to the admission into the worshipping community of those normally regarded as outsiders. 66.18-21 in fact goes further in this direction than does 56.3-8 in that it envisages the admission of those not of Israelite stock to be priests and Levites (66.21). The notable correspondence between 56.1-8 and 66.18-24 suggests that they have been deliberately placed in their present position to form a framework for the entire collection of oracles in 56–66, whatever their original provenance may have been. In short, the internal evidence of the chapters themselves suggests that far from their being a haphazard medley of oracles there is a degree of sophistication in the intricate structure of their final form.

The following diagram illustrates the broadly symmetrical structure of chs. 56–66:

56.1-8 concerning sabbath-keeping and admission to worship
56.9-12 denunciation of leaders who 'turn to their own way'
57.1–58.14 denunciation of idolatry; promise to the faithful
59.1-15a lament on behalf of the community
59.15b-20 the divine warrior intervenes
60–62 promises of salvation
63.1-6 the divine warrior intervenes
63.7–64.12 lament on behalf of the community
65.1-25 denunciation of idolatry; promise to the faithful
66.3-4 denunciation of those who 'choose their own ways'
66.1-24 concerning temple, sacrifice, admission to worship

For discussion of Westermann's detailed analysis, based on this remarkable structural symmetry, of the probable chronological relationship of the various literary units and of the process by which these chapters reached their present form see pp. 63-67.

Literary Forms and Poetic Imagery

One of the particularly interesting features of Third Isaiah is not only that a variety of literary forms appear in these chapters but also that they provide evidence of how traditional forms were forced into new directions to suit the requirements of a changing historical situation. Some of the oracles in their form and expression resemble the sayings of pre-exilic prophets so closely that it is difficult to judge whether they are pre-exilic in origin and have been reapplied to a later situation, or whether they are postexilic formulations modelled on the sayings of earlier prophets (e.g. 56.9-12). In other instances, however, it is clear that traditional forms have taken a new direction due to the exigencies of the new situation which prevailed after the exile and the changes it brought to the life of the community—in particular, the tensions which threatened to divide it. It is here that these chapters as a whole are most clearly distinguishable from the pre-exilic prophets.

The following is not intended as an exhaustive treatment of the literary forms of Isaiah 56–66; rather its aim is to highlight some of the areas in which development can be seen. I begin with a consideration of the judgment oracles, for it is in these that we come closest to the forms of expression in which the prophets of pre-exilic times couched their messages; yet at the same time we can detect a breakdown of traditional forms.

Judgment Oracles

1. *Isaiah 56.9-12*
This passage is a masterly example of a prophetic oracle of judgment, comprising the two traditional elements, pronouncement of judgment and grounds of accusation. In its uncompromising denunciation of ineffectual leadership, and the powerful imagery with which it castigates the betrayal of responsibility by those who seek their own gain rather than the community's well-being, it is a superb example of this literary form. Its figurative language has certain reminiscences of Ezekiel's indictment of Israel's leaders (34.1-10), but its brevity is in marked contrast to Ezekiel's extended metaphor. On the basis of 'form, style and diction' Westermann is convinced that Isaiah 56.9-12 is not only couched in the earlier form but is pre-exilic in origin. It is, however, notoriously difficult to establish priority on literary grounds, and the

possibility of postexilic origin cannot be excluded. Although in general the messages of the postexilic prophets evince a dependence on their predecessors in the great age of prophecy, the possibility of a resurgence for a time of the spirit and power of authentic prophecy cannot be ruled out. Either way, whatever the date of origin, the inclusion here of this judgment oracle gives an insight into the situation in Judah after the return from exile and the deplorable state of some, at any rate, of its leadership. The kaleidoscopic imagery in which the denunciation is couched reflects the multifarious sins of which the leaders are guilty.

What kind of leadership is castigated is not entirely clear: both religious and political leaders may be included. 'Watchman' is a term which generally signifies a prophet (Jer. 6.17; Ezek. 3.17; 33.7) whereas 'shepherd' refers frequently to political leadership (Jer. 23.1-4; Ezek. 34.1-10, especially v. 4). The accusation is comprehensive. At first it is the ignorance of the watchmen, their failure to realize the dangers of the situation and to alert the community to an appropriate response, which is at issue. They are quiet as sleeping dogs murmuring in their dreams (*hōzīm*, a word occurring only here which has the sense 'to talk confusedly'). This is no conventional imagery but comes straight from observation of nature. But then the accusation changes. Dogs, all dogs, have ravenous, insatiable appetites, and so do the shepherds of Israel, intent on their own advantage, with never a thought beyond the pleasure of the present moment as they sing their drinking songs, behaving arrogantly as if the future were at their disposal not the Lord's. The pattern of the metaphors is deliberately chiastic; the newly coined metaphors of dumb and ravenous dogs, the former useless, the latter dangerous, serve to illuminate the conventional expressions of 'watchmen' and 'shepherds', and to provide the transition between them. These are the depths to which the community's leaders have sunk. In terms reminiscent of a curse formula (cf. Deut. 28.26), wild beasts are summoned to work destruction (see also Jer. 12.9-10 where also the context concerns shepherds who have failed in their trust). This, too, is figurative language, and it is a confusion of the poetic with prosaic reality to attempt to explain the particular form of this curse in terms of the threat of battle where those slain will be devoured by wild beasts, as does Westermann. It is, however, important to notice the difference in tone here from the way in which Ezekiel, in his condemnation of Israel's shepherds, makes reference to wild beasts (34.5, 8). In Ezekiel the words are descriptive of the fate which has already befallen Israel; in Isa. 56.9 we have the pronouncement, indeed the solemn summons, of future judgment. The impact of the whole is heightened by a play on the word 'come' (*'ētāyū*, an uncommon word) at the beginning and end of the section which binds together the pronouncement of judgment and the accusation: 'All you wild beasts, *come* to eat...' (v. 9); '*come*...let us drink', say the shepherds (v. 12), revelling in sensual pleasure.

2. *Isaiah 57.3-13*
This second judgment oracle differs from the previous one not only in the subject of its accusation, which this time is not the leaders but apparently the community at large or at any rate a section of society (see below), but also in the nature of the charges brought and in its literary form. The summons to 'draw near hither' (v. 3), together with the formulation as a series of questions (vv. 4-6), distinguish it as a 'trial speech'. Its purpose differs, however, from the trial speeches of Second Isaiah where it is the nations and their gods who are summoned by Yahweh to enter into a lawsuit with him that he may prove his claim to sole sovereignty (cf. 41.1-4; 45.20-21). In some respects Isaiah 57 has a resemblance to Malachi 1 where God's indictment of the nation is set out in a similar series of questions.

The manner in which the cultic irregularities are described as adultery and prostitution (possibly with a literal as well as a figurative sense) resonates with similar pre-exilic utterances (e.g. Hos. 1.2; 2.4; 4.13; Jer. 2.20; Ezek. 16.15-22). The reference to child sacrifice, too, would not be out of place especially in later pre-exilic times (2 Kgs 23.10; Jer. 7.31). There is, however, no consensus as to the origins of this judgment oracle. Westermann unhesitatingly attributes it to the pre-exilic period; Whybray equally confidently maintains that there is no reason to suppose it is not postexilic. Nevertheless it is clear from its inclusion in this collection of oracles that it had a relevance to the situation in postexilic Judah.

Whereas vv. 3-13a consist entirely of accusation and judgment, it becomes apparent from the framework within which the indictment is set (vv.1-2, 13b) that there is a division within society between the righteous and the wayward. This framework, as Westermann notes, is decidedly liturgical in tone, both in the lament of v. 1 (cf. Ps. 12.1) and in the assurance of v. 13b. A similar juxtaposition of lament and judgment oracle is to be found in Mic. 7.1-4. It is in this juxtaposition of the liturgical with a prophetic oracle of judgment that we gain an insight into the compilation of the material. As divisions increased within the postexilic community earlier prophetic oracles were reapplied to those who were now regarded as pre-eminently the transgressors.

The question remains: who were regarded as such? Various answers have been given. Some commentators would relate the condemnation to the whole community, others to the semi-pagan, syncretistic worship practised by those who had remained in Palestine amid the Canaanite population during the years of exile, when the exigencies of the time may well have caused them to turn for security to other deities and to illegitimate religious practices including necromancy (v. 9). Others go yet further in this direction, seeing here words of accusation levelled by those who had returned from exile against the other section of the community, and thus evidence of dissension within the community. For the very different view proposed by P.D. Hanson see the discussion on p. 89. In the terminology used there are unmistakable links with earlier chapters of the book of Isaiah: the designation 'sons of the sorceress' (*'ōneⁿāh*, v. 3) is paralleled in Isa. 2.6 (cf. also Mic. 5.11; Jer. 27.9), and the offensive gestures of ridicule are not unlike those condemned in Isa. 37.23. The exact nature both of the judgment and of the specific religious activity condemned in v. 6 is unclear. Whatever its meaning, its impact would undoubtedly have been heightened by the play on the words 'smooth [sc. stones]' (*ḥalleqē*) and 'your portion' (*ḥelqēk*). There is irony, too, both in the scathing accusation and in the pronouncement of judgment. The 'high and lofty mountain' (*har-gāboah wᵉnissa'*) which is the scene of Israel's adultery against God recalls the 'high mountain' (*har-gāboah*; 40.9) where the good news of God's saving action was to be proclaimed to, or by, Zion (the Hebrew is ambiguous). Moreover, vv. 12-13 are replete with irony: the God who has held his peace for so long (v. 11) will break the silence to 'tell of your righteousness and your doings, but they will not help you'. Their idols are treated with contempt. They do not merit even a name:

> When you cry out, let your collection of idols [lit. collected
> things] deliver you!
> The wind will carry them off,
> a breath will take them away.

3. *Isaiah 58.1-14*
This passage is of particular interest both from the form-critical viewpoint and for the insight it gives into the problems and religious attitudes of the postexilic community in Judah (on which see Chapter 6). In form it is remarkably different from the two previous oracles of judgment discussed above. Yet it seems appropriate to include it here since this passage, and this alone, opens with a categorical summons to the prophet to bring an indictment against the people for their sin in the style of the pre-exilic prophets (cf. Hos. 8.1; Mic. 3.8). This opening summons leads us to expect an oracle of judgment as stern in its denunciation as anything in those earlier prophets. The reality turns out to be otherwise. A surprising change of tone follows. Of the two traditional elements—accusation and pronouncement of judgment—the former appears briefly in vv. 3b-4a; the latter is entirely absent. The rest of the passage consists of a series of exhortations followed by conditional promises of blessing. It is here, in this breakdown of the conventional form of the judgment oracle, that the contrast with earlier prophets is most apparent. Stylistically the closest parallel is to be found in the speeches of Job's friends (Job 11.13-19). The form is highly complex and perhaps best described as 'symptomatic of the coming together of prophetic and liturgical speech' (Westermann).

Following immediately on the divine authorization of the prophet as a messenger of judgment (contrast 61.1 where he is commissioned to proclaim salvation) there is a parenthetical description of the outward piety of the community (vv. 2-3a), a people who lament that their practice of fasting is ineffectual and secures no response from God. It is clear from this, as well as from the language in which the promises of blessing are couched, that the community, or the section of it addressed, is conscious of some kind of distress and lack of well-being, probably attributable to the disappointment of hopes raised by the promises of Second Isaiah. The responsibility is laid firmly at the community's door. Despite their outward religious observances there is only apparent, not actual, commitment to righteous action and to obedience to God's commandments (v. 2). The thought is similar to 59.1-2, 'your iniquities have separated between you and your God'.

A comparison of this passage with ch. 58 is instructive. Whereas 59.1 is followed by powerful denunciation, ch. 58 is, in general, exhortatory in tone. Only in vv. 3b-4 is there anything in the way of direct accusation. The marked difference between this and the exhortatory character of the rest of the chapter is at its clearest in the contrast between vv. 3b and 13 which are alike in using the expression 'to seek your own pleasure' but are remarkably different in tone. The additional fact that the accusation in vv. 3b-4 is concerned with the oppressive treatment of workers and the aggressive pursuit of wealth and not, as in vv. 6-7, with criticism of the traditional observance of fasting, suggests that the chapter is not a unity but has been expanded at a later stage to meet the needs of a fresh situation.

The central section itself (vv. 6-12) falls into two parts. The first (vv. 6-9a) is focused directly on the question of fasting, reinterpreting it radically in terms of positive social action on behalf of the disadvantaged in society; the second (vv. 9b-12) uses similar terms in speaking of social obligation and is identical in form, being a conditional promise of blessing, but has no specific reference to fasting. It should be noted, too, that whereas vv. 1-6 and 13-14 have the form of divine speech, the intervening verses refer to Yahweh in the third person. The

concluding section (vv. 13-14), although consistent with the
preceding verses in structure as a conditional promise, in tone
as an exhortation, and in subject matter as concerned with a
religious institution, in this instance the sabbath, nevertheless
differs remarkably in its attitude. There is here no radical
attempt to reinterpret traditional forms of sabbath observance
but a reaffirmation of customary practice with no apparent
acknowledgement of any social dimension. As remarked
above (p. 17), Westermann associates this concluding injunction of ch. 58 with the similarly strong emphasis on the sabbath in 56.3-8, and argues that the two form a framework to
what originally existed as an independent complex of
tradition.

Finally, it should be noted that this chapter shows some
signs of the influence of Wisdom circles. Not only are the
conditional promises similar in form to the speeches of
Job's friends, as noted already, but there is, according to
Westermann, a hint of 'the ridicule of the rationalist' in the
satirical expression 'to bow down one's head like a rush' (v. 5).
Verse 14, too, which unlike v. 13 is couched in traditional language, draws on Job 22.26 together with Deut. 32.13.

Laments

Isaiah 59.1-15a; 63.7–64.12

These two laments, which counterbalance each other so
appropriately in the overall symmetry of the structure of
Third Isaiah, differ considerably in their literary form. Of the
two, that in 63.7–64.12 is the more traditional in structure,
and it is generally agreed that it originated in the early exilic
period, though Muilenburg notes that it lacks the grim detail
of much of the book of Lamentations which belongs to that
period, and suggests a time rather later in the exile when
bitter memories had begun to fade. Its powerful images and its
authentic expression of emotion are so impressive that
Westermann describes it as 'probably the most powerful
psalm of communal lamentation in the Bible'. It follows the
conventional pattern of such laments within the psalter, consisting of the usual elements: recollection of God's past saving

actions (63.7-14) (extended as in Psalm 89 which not only begins similarly but likewise concludes by questioning of God); plea for help, which includes a description of the distress which was the immediate cause of the lament (63.15–64.5a); and confession of sin (64.5b-7). Finally the various elements in the lament are gathered up (64.8-12), culminating in the anguished questioning of God, characteristic of the lament form:

> Wilt thou restrain thyself at these things, O Lord?
> Wilt thou keep silent, and afflict us sorely?

The lament gives the impression of a deliberate symmetry in its structure characterized by a certain amount of repetition:

63.15	plea for God's intervention	64.1
63.16	claim upon God as father	64.8
63.17	acknowledgement of sin	64.5b-7
63.18-19	reason for the lament	64.11

Finally, the whole is bound together by the corresponding questions concerning the inactivity of God with which the lament begins and ends (63.15 and 64.12). The passage is also of particular interest for its use of the expression 'holy spirit' (vv. 10-11) which occurs only once elsewhere in the Old Testament in Psalm 51.11 (MT 13), a great penitential psalm of the individual.

Unlike 63.7–64.12 which follows the conventional form of a communal lament, ch. 59 is an interesting example of departure from traditional forms. Westermann terms it 'a most curious and odd creation' in that it contains elements not germane to the lament form. In fact, so much does it depart from the conventional lament form that the question has been raised whether it is right to classify it as a lament. Scholars are divided on this form-critical question, some preferring to treat the passage as a liturgy in which a prophetic voice mingles with a communal lament (Haller, Muilenburg), others as a sermon (Kessler), a matter which is discussed below.

The opening words, introduced as they are by the particle 'behold', are to be understood as the prophet's response to an unrecorded lament by the people, perplexed by the failure of

Yahweh to intervene and by his apparent disregard of their prayers. The problem, says the prophet, lies not in any limitation of Yahweh's power. It is the result of sin, their own sins, which have raised a barrier between themselves and God. The accusation in vv. 2-3 is as sharp as anything in the pre-exilic prophets (cf. Isa. 1.15); but, in place of the announcement of punishment which traditionally accompanied the accusation, the direct address to the hearers soon passes over into a description of their sin, its impact heightened by the striking poetic imagery (vv. 5-6). It is this descriptive aspect of the material which gives the passage something of a sermonic character since it constitutes an explanation to a despondent people rather than an accusation. The sins referred to here are social injustices not cultic irregularities—the insidious evils by which justice is perverted in the law courts, and the more blatant crimes of violence and murder.

Two strands seem to be intertwined, the community's lament and the prophetic voice—hence the characterization of the passage by some as a prophetic liturgy. The chapter falls into three distinct sections: first, the prophet's response to a communal lament which vindicates Yahweh by way of accusing the people (vv. 1-8); secondly, the ensuing lament, by or on behalf of the people, which includes confession of sin (v. 12; an unusual feature in the traditional form of judgment oracle) and admits the truth of the accusation (vv. 9-15a); thirdly, the assurance of God's intervention to save those who repent (vv. 15b-20; for a similarly abrupt transition to words of assurance compare Joel 2.18). Yahweh is portrayed here as the warrior God who avenges those who 'turn from transgression' (v. 20; cf. 42.13; 52.10). A similar pattern of community lament followed by Yahweh's epiphany is to be found in Psalm 60. The two sections, lament (1-15a) and epiphany (15b-20) are linked together. Yahweh takes action precisely because he sees that there is no justice (v. 15; cf. vv. 9 and 11). The salvation which was far from them (v. 11) is seen to be at hand when he intervenes. Here the divine will is manifested to see right done for the despairing and oppressed. The reference to the coastlands (v. 18) and to the acknowledgement of Yahweh's name from east and west suggests that in origin this portrayal of the divine warrior was concerned with foreign enemies, as is clearly the case in 63.1-6. However, as ch. 59 now stands, the old antithesis of Israel and her enemies has been translated, in the new situation existing after the exile, into the antithesis of righteous and transgressors within the community itself. In this way traditional language is turned in a new direction to address the circumstances of an increasingly divided community. The concern now is not with external enemies but with destructive forces within the Jewish community.

The debate as to the literary form of the passage is not easily settled. Whybray profoundly disagrees both with those who regard the passage as a prophetic liturgy and with those who classify it as sermonic. He takes issue with the former on two main grounds: first, that the passage is a literary compilation, not an intrinsic unity, for the situation implied in vv. 1-8 and 9-15a, all of which are addressed to the whole community, is not the same as that in vv. 15b-20 where there is clear evidence of internal divisions; and secondly, on the theological grounds that 'it is difficult to conceive of a liturgy in which the simple confession of sin in vv. 12-13 would be regarded as sufficient to cancel the effect of the extremely grave sins condemned in vv. 1-4 and so to open the way for the joyful promise of vv. 15b-20'. He finds serious problems, too, with the view that the passage constitutes a sermon addressed to people perplexed by their pitiable plight, not least because of the long liturgical prayer which is incorporated into it. He regards vv. 5-8 as, in all probability, 'a rhetorical "embellishment" added subsequently to a piece which was originally not primarily a condemnation, whether prophetic or sermonic, but a disputation in which the speaker gave reasons for God's apparent inactivity'. The debate on literary form apart, there can be little disagreement about the power of the poetic imagery, and Muilenburg's comment that 'few chapters in the Bible are so rich and diverse in their vocabulary of sin' is surely appropriate.

Portrayal of the Divine Warrior

Isaiah 59.15b-20; 63.1-6

There are interesting, and significant, contrasts between the portrayal of the divine warrior in these two passages. As was noted above, 59.15b-20 provides an illustration of the way in which traditional motifs have been reinterpreted for new situations. What originally concerned Yahweh's intervention against foreign enemies has now been directed against internal adversaries. In this respect this passage differs from 63.1-6. The chief point of both passages, however, is the fact not only of Yahweh's initiative but of his sole action in the defeat of evil (59.16; 63.5).

In 63.1-6 the prophet makes use of a secular form familiar to his hearers—the customary summons of a watchman to an approaching stranger to identify himself—but the content is based on the motif of the divine warrior. Yahweh is not named, but the identification is clear (cf. Isa. 5.1-7). Fresh from his victory he announces that 'right has won the day' (NEB). Although the specific reference to Edom and Bozrah (v. 1) has sometimes been queried since the passage is concerned with the nations as a whole, its similarity to Isa. 34.6 where Bozrah and Edom are symbolic of hostile nations supports its authenticity here (cf. also Ps. 137.7; Obad. 13–14; Lam. 4.21-22). This is the most extreme statement within Isaiah 56–66 of opposition to the nations in defence of Israel.

Oracles of both Judgment and Salvation

Isaiah 65.8-16

It has been noted above that the judgment oracle in 57.3-13 is now set within a framework consisting of vv. 1-2 and v. 13b, an arrangement which has the effect of transforming it secondarily into an oracle both of judgment and salvation. In contrast, 65.8-16 is intrinsically an oracle both of judgment and of salvation, addressed respectively to two opposing factions within the community. In this dual orientation it differs in a remarkable fashion from the traditional forms of pre-exilic prophecy in which the nation is treated as a corporate entity whether for judgment or for salvation. In its present form ch. 65 as a whole is symmetrical in structure: vv. 1-7 consist entirely of accusation against idolaters; vv. 8-16a set out the contrasting destiny of two disparate groups within the community, detailing the blessings in store for the one ('my servants' vv. 13-14, 'my chosen' v. 15) and the sorrows which await the other; vv. 16b-25 are purely a description of blessing. These diverse sections are held together by the theme of call and response which is reiterated in vv. 1, 12 and 24. Nevertheless it is difficult to say whether there is an intrinsic connection between vv. 1-16a and 16b-23, for the latter in contrast to the former contains a number of reminiscences of Second Isaiah which link it also with chs. 60–62.

The present position of the chapter suggests that it is intended as God's response to the lament about the silence of God with which ch. 64 ends. Nevertheless it is unlikely that there is an integral connection between the two. The central concern of ch. 65 is with the deep division within the community between those who, from this perspective at any rate, are regarded as faithful worshippers of Yahweh and their opponents who are considered by them to be apostate. It is to this latter group that the oracle is addressed from v. 11 onwards as a pronouncement of judgment. The evils condemned here are cultic irregularities, though they differ in important respects from those to which 57.3-10 refer.

Further Reading

On literary structure and compilation:
Jones, *Isaiah 56–66 and Joel*, p. 33.
Westermann, *Isaiah 40–66*, pp. 296-308.

The following will also be found helpful:
R. Abramowski, 'Zum literarischen Problem von Jes. 56–66', *Theologische Studien und Kritiken* 96–97 (1925), pp. 90-143.
H. Odeburg, *Trito-Isaiah (Isaiah lvi-lxvi): A Literary and Linguistic Analysis* (Uppsala, 1931).
R. Rendtorff, 'Zur Komposition des Buches Jesaja', *VT* 34 (1984),

pp. 295-320.
On poetic form:
Muilenburg, *Isaiah Chapters 40-66*, pp. 417-18, 652-773.

In addition:
J. Blenkinsopp, 'Second Isaiah—Prophet of Universalism', *JSOT* 41
(1988), pp. 83-103 has a useful discussion of ch. 56 from the standpoint of form criticism.

3

THIRD ISAIAH AND
THE CANONICAL BOOK

The Unity of the Book of Isaiah

THE ARGUMENTS FOR the traditional threefold division of the book of Isaiah into what are, broadly speaking, eighth-century, exilic and postexilic sections are familiar enough to make discussion here unnecessary. The differences in historical setting and in the issues which had to be addressed in these several periods of prophetic ministry must be appreciated if the meaning and relevance of the text are to be understood. At the same time it has to be remembered that the book in its final canonical form is a unity, and this too must be taken fully into account. In what sense prophetic material from such widely different periods can be accounted a unity has increasingly become the subject of recent scholarly discussion.

The presence of exilic and postexilic material in the book of Isaiah, whose title identifies it as 'the vision' of an eighth-century prophet, can hardly be due to a mere accident of history. There are far too many connections in both thought and language between chs. 1–39 and the later chapters for this to be an adequate explanation. Even less satisfactory is the suggestion that the book is the result of nothing more than the practical expedient of filling an incomplete scroll. A more satisfactory explanation, and one which has been widely adopted, suggests that the long continuity of the Isaiah tradition is to be attributed to a school of disciples. This hypothesis would enable us both to explain the unity of the book and also

to account for the difference in historical setting of the various
sections. These followers or disciples are held to have cherished the message of the great eighth-century prophet,
transmitting and reapplying it to later circumstances which
were inevitably very different from those of Isaiah's time. This
view is associated primarily with the name of Mowinckel, and
it still finds considerable support, as the bibliography at the end
of this chapter indicates. More recently, however, this theory
too has been challenged and found wanting, on the grounds
that it fails to account sufficiently for the highly complex
nature of chs. 1–39 themselves. Not only do these chapters
include some of the latest of all the Isaiah oracles, in particular
the apocalyptic material in chs. 24–27; recent research has
further demonstrated the possibility that their present structure may be the result of later editing carried out in the light of
the concerns of postexilic Judaism, perhaps by those who were
responsible for the collection of oracles in chs. 56–66.

Among the foremost critics of this view, that the transmission of the Isaiah tradition from the eighth century to postexilic times was due to the continued existence over the centuries of a group of disciples, is R.E. Clements. His doubts arise
both from scepticism about the existence of a school or group
of disciples for which there is so little firm evidence, and also
from concern over the use of the word 'disciple' in this context:
in view of the long period of time envisaged, this term becomes
virtually meaningless. Rather, the connection between chs. 1–
39 and the exilic and postexilic material which comprises
Second and Third Isaiah respectively is to be regarded,
Clements argues, not as the result of a process merely of sup-
plementation in which successive layers of material were
added over a period of time, but rather in terms of a redactional unity created with the urgent needs of the postexilic
community in mind. Clements points out a number of passages within chs. 1–39 which show evidence of the influence
of other passages in the book, particularly chs. 40–55. Among
these he includes not only ch. 35, a passage which had already
for some time been regarded as in essence a summary of
Second Isaiah's message of hope, but also, for similar reasons,
11.12-16; 19.23 and 27.12-13.

The evidence of influence such as this leads Clements to the conclusion that

> the conjunction of the prophecies of chapter 40 and those following with those that precede them was a deliberate step taken by the scribal redactors of the book for a profoundly religious reason. It had nothing to do with matters of literary convenience or assumed identity of authorship but was designed to clarify and fill out the divine message given to Israel, and especially to Jerusalem.

He argues similarly for an integral, rather than a merely superficial, unity between Second and Third Isaiah. Chapters 56–66 were intended, he believes, 'not as a fresh and entirely self-contained declaration from Yahweh to the postexilic community, but rather as a carrying forward of the divine word as it had been declared on the eve of the overthrow of Babylon by the unnamed prophet of 40–55'.

A unity of the kind which Clements envisages is more fundamental and of altogether greater significance than a merely external connection produced simply by the addition of exilic and postexilic material to Isaiah's message. Not only do the later chapters contain echoes of the thought and language of First Isaiah so that only in the light of this can their imagery be properly appreciated, but the reverse is also true: chs. 1–39 themselves can only be adequately understood when it is recognized that the entire book has been edited with the needs of postexilic Judaism in mind.

Instances of Redactional Unity

There are, indeed, such remarkable similarities in the concerns of chs. 1 and 65–66 and in the imagery which they use, that M.A. Sweeney describes them as a redactional 'envelope' which binds the whole book together into a unity, whether or not they were actually composed for that purpose. The points of resemblance are too numerous to be discussed in detail here, but the following are among those noted by Sweeney. The denunciation of idolatrous practices in 65.3 is comparable to that in 1.29-31, and both, significantly, refer to 'gardens' as the location where such practices were carried on (cf. also 66.17).

Likewise 65.12 shares with 1.11 and 29 the theme of false choice, choosing (*bāḥar*) that in which the worshippers themselves, not God, delight (*ḥāpeṣ*; cf. 66.3). The figurative language used in 65.22, in which the days of God's chosen ones are compared to the days of a tree, may be seen as a deliberate contrast with the rotten tree in 1.30-31 which symbolizes those who were guilty of apostasy. In particular the imagery of 1.29-31 seems to permeate chs. 65–66.

The resemblances between chs. 1 and 65–66 have been examined in detail also by Liebreich. In the light of so many features in common he suggests that it is this deliberate correspondence between chs. 1 and 66 which may explain the strangely negative note of judgment with which the book of Isaiah ends, a feature the more surprising in that it comes as an unexpected anti-climax after the positive tone of 66.18-23. In both 1.31 and 66.24 divine judgment is represented as 'unquenchable fire', and thus a deliberate link is established between the beginning and end of the book. The occurrence of the word 'to rebel' (*pāšaʿ*) in 1.2 and 66.24 should also be noted. The many other links between chs. 1 and 65–66 are usefully tabulated by Liebreich. Among more general features which serve the purpose of binding together the entire book of Isaiah Liebreich singles out the three occurrences of the expression, 'Hear the word of the Lord', which occur, significantly, at the beginning (1.10), middle (39.5) and end (66.5) of the book. We may note in addition a number of other connections between First and Third Isaiah. The promise of 62.4, 'Your land shall no more be termed Desolate', is a conscious reversal of the historical situation described in 1.7, and 60.1 seems to echo 9.2 in its confident assurance to Zion that 'your light has come'. The composite quotation of 11.6 and 9 in 65.25 is significant as an indication that the new heavens and new earth of 65.17-25 are to be understood as the fulfilment of an earlier promise. And surely the reference to Yahweh as 'high and lifted up' in 57.15 is a deliberate reminiscence of Isaiah's call vision (6.1).

It becomes increasingly apparent that if we are to have a proper appreciation of the book of Isaiah we must not overlook the fact that it has been deliberately forged into a redactional unity. It has proved to be an unfortunate consequence of

Duhm's work that the importance of seeing the book as a whole has tended to be obscured. His analytical approach undoubtedly made an important contribution to sharpening our perception of the different historical context of the later chapters of Isaiah, but it also had the negative result of diverting attention from the final form of the book. Historical issues have tended to take pride of place, and the importance of literary context and of the interrelationship of the various sections of the book has as a result been somewhat overlooked. C.R. Seitz has given a timely reminder that biblical scholarship is concerned with more than simply the historical context of the original message: 'our study of Isaiah, as of other parts of the Old Testament, is deficient if it stops short at the historical; for Isaiah's word is no historic artifact, but a lively and relentless challenge to the modern world'. Nevertheless, Seitz does not minimize the importance of recognizing the diverse historical origins of 'the three Isaiahs', for he sees in this diversity a salutary reminder that the message of the prophets was grounded in specific circumstances and was of immediate relevance to their own society with its particular concerns. Yet to read the book as a whole is to acknowledge that the message did not die when those circumstances had passed, for had this been so it would merely have spoken 'a restricted word to generations now long gone'. The unity for which Seitz contends is not that of single authorship or of uniform historical setting. It is theological, and is to be found in 'the common witness of all sixty-six chapters to the one God of Israel, Isaiah's "Holy One"'.

To conclude, the message of Third Isaiah must be considered in its own right as a prophetic word, but it must also be understood in relation to the whole canonical book of Isaiah. To regard it as simply an appendix to the words of greater predecessors is to devalue it and to mute its challenge. It is encouraging that scholarly trends in recent years have begun to redress the balance and to focus fresh interest on chs. 56–66.

The Interrelationship of Second and Third Isaiah

No reader of the book of Isaiah can fail to be struck by the many points of similarity between chs. 40–55 and 56–66. They have in common not only several themes but also many forms of expression which in some instances are virtually identical. Naturally the question arises as to what the relationship between them is. Is the message of Third Isaiah the product of a second-rate prophet who can do little more than echo the message of an outstanding predecessor, or is this an example of the creative transmission of an earlier prophetic word to meet the needs of a changed situation? The relationship is, in fact, a far more complex one than might appear at first glance, for in spite of the many similarities there are notable differences both in tone and in perspective. Not only are there oracles of judgment (e.g. 56.9–57.13; 59.1-8) in which Third Isaiah is more akin to the pre-exilic prophets than to Second Isaiah (though cf. 43.22-24), but there are other less obvious differences, shifts in meaning of a more subtle kind but none the less significant. Where Second Isaiah looks for a dramatic saving action on God's part to restore his people to their homeland, for Third Isaiah the return from exile is largely over, and the community he addresses, re-establishing itself in its homeland, is impoverished and disillusioned. Its life is disrupted, too, by internal factions (66.5). Consequently in chs. 56–66 Second Isaiah's familiar designation of Israel as 'servant' of the Lord is abandoned, and instead we find this term only in the plural (56.6; 63.17; 65.8, 9, 13 [3א], 14, 15; 66.14; cf. 54.17), for the tensions which threaten to destroy the community make it no longer possible to speak in this way of the population as a whole but only of the faithful group within it. The optimistic promises of Second Isaiah have given way to a new and depressing situation in which the excitement of expectancy has been lost in the disappointment of unfulfilled hopes. Where this later prophet quotes the words of his predecessor it is not mere imitation but adaptation of the message to meet the urgent needs of the time, and in addressing his contemporaries he has shaped the message from his own particular perspective.

We shall now look in greater detail at the close connections which exist between Second and Third Isaiah, and also at the difference in tone and perspective which so clearly distinguishes them.

Reminiscences of Second Isaiah

Just as the first and last chapters of the entire book of Isaiah are linked by several common features of thought and expression, so it is of interest to note that the theme of 'comfort' with which Second Isaiah begins (40.1) recurs in the final chapter of Third Isaiah (66.13). There are a number of other obvious connections. The prophet's confident assurance amid the community's despair that 'the Lord's hand is not shortened, that it cannot save' (59.1), seems intended as a deliberate reminiscence of 50.2. This is also true of the emphatic assertion, included in both of the divine warrior passages, that God acts alone in salvation without human assistance: 'he saw that there was no man, and wondered that there was no one to intervene' (59.16; cf. 63.5)—though this could also be seen as a possible rejoinder to Second Isaiah's perception of Cyrus as God's agent in the deliverance of his people. Likewise the words of divine authority which undergird the renewal of the ancient patriarchal promise in 60.22, 'I am the Lord; in its time I will hasten it', could hardly fail to call to mind the promise in 49.23, 'Those who wait for me shall not be put to shame', prefaced as it is by the statement, 'then you shall know that I am the Lord'.

Several of Second Isaiah's characteristic themes are present also in Third Isaiah, among them the idea of the pilgrimage of the nations to Jerusalem. Second and Third Isaiah are alike in envisaging this as the means not only of bringing home Israel's scattered people (60.3; cf. 49.22) but of filling Jerusalem with vast resources from other lands to beautify Yahweh's city and temple (60.5, 11; cf. 45.14), a purpose in striking contrast to 2.2-3 where the nations come to Zion to seek instruction and the word of the Lord. In both Second and

Third Isaiah we also find the motif of reversal, whereby future blessing mirrors and counterbalances past deprivation: Israel, the forsaken wife (62.4; cf. 49.21; 50.1; 54.6) is restored to favour, the oppressed are honoured, their oppressors paying them homage, and, in Third Isaiah, being actively engaged in Jerusalem's restoration (60.10). However, the particularly harsh attitude shown towards other nations in 45.14 and above all in 49.26 is not present to the same extent in Third Isaiah. The only comparable instance occurs in 60.12 which is widely regarded as a secondary interpolation. A comparison of 60.14 with the similar but harsher tone of 49.23 sufficiently illustrates this point.

The language in which Second Isaiah describes the servant figure has such unmistakable echoes in 61.1-3 (cf. particularly 42.1 and 49.9), a passage which is generally taken to refer to the commissioning of the prophet for his ministry, that a number of earlier commentators suggested that this passage should be regarded as one of the Servant Songs and attributed to Second Isaiah (see W.W. Cannon for a list of the parallels to Second Isaiah). However, the resemblance must not be exaggerated, nor should comparison be restricted to the Servant Songs. The language of anointing recalls the Elijah/Elisha narrative in 1 Kgs 19.16 (cf. also Ps. 105.15 where the term 'prophets' is used in parallel to 'my anointed ones'), and the links with 2 Sam. 23.1-4 and Mic. 3.8 should also be noted.

One of the most striking of the themes serving to link Second and Third Isaiah is the extended imagery of Jerusalem personified as a woman, which forms a feminine counterpart to the servant figure of Second Isaiah. Several times throughout the book of Isaiah Jerusalem is called 'daughter of Zion' (1.8; 3.16; 10.32; 16.1; 37.22; 52.2; 62.11). The imagery is not, however, restricted to those passages where this specific designation occurs. J.F.A. Sawyer has argued that these passages together form a series of dramatic poems which recount the story of a woman's life from a time of bereavement and barrenness (49.14-21) until eventually she gives birth to a son (66.7). Sometimes the woman is named as Zion or Jerusalem or is clearly identified with the city by reference to her gates, walls or builders; at other times, like the servant of Second Isaiah, her identity remains ambiguous. In the latter part of her story as it is related in chs. 56–66, the nations bring gifts to her (including gold and frankincense; 60.6), her wedding is celebrated and her erstwhile names 'forsaken' and 'desolate' are changed, for Yahweh rejoices over her 'as the bridegroom rejoices over the bride' (62.5). Ultimately sons are born to her (66.7-9)—metaphorical language which continues in 66.12 with its reference to feeding, carrying on the hip and dandling on the knees. Only at one point is the sequence disrupted when the city is described as a whore (57.6-13; cf. 1.21-26). The culmination of the story in the birth of sons is a reiteration of Second Isaiah's promise in 54.1-3 (cf. 49.19-21). Yet, in spite of this connection, there is a noticeable difference in context. Whereas in Second Isaiah the point at issue was the necessary increase in population to ensure the survival and adequate defence of the community, in 66.7-9 the language of birth serves as an expression of the miraculous nature of God's activity. There is in this description of painless birth, Sawyer suggests, a deliberate reversal of Gen. 3.26. Yahweh himself is pictured as the midwife in attendance on this supernatural birth of the nation, the verb 'to bring to birth' (*hišbīr*) being a technical term for the midwife's task.

Third Isaiah's Distinctive Outlook

At first sight ch. 56 seems to follow smoothly from ch. 55. There is no indication of any kind of break between them. Yet it soon becomes clear that the concerns of this prophet differ considerably from those of Second Isaiah. There are matters of worship and religious observance to be considered (ch. 58); and there are disputes about those entitled to participate (ch. 56) and the importance or otherwise of the Jerusalem temple to be settled (66.1). Nevertheless ch. 56 itself begins with words strongly reminiscent of 46.13: both alike announce the imminence of salvation and deliverance. Yet here we encounter immediately that element of both continuity and discontinuity with Second Isaiah which is apparent in varying degrees throughout these chapters. In fact, in some instances it is the

striking similarity of expression itself, recalling as it does the
message of Second Isaiah, which throws into relief the
significant change of tone. A comparison of 46.13 with 56.1
illustrates the point. Second Isaiah's words emphasize
Yahweh and his direct intervention: 'I bring near my deliverance... I will put salvation in Zion'. In 56.1, in contrast, the
directness of expression is muted by the use first of an intran-
sitive then of a passive verb: 'my salvation will come, and my
deliverance be revealed'. A similar change from the directness
of Second Isaiah's style is apparent, too, when 65.17 is compared with 43.18. Both speak of God's radically new action (in
65.17 in eschatological terms) which supersedes and renders
superfluous the recollection of 'former things'; but once again
the direct address of Second Isaiah's imperatives, 'Remember
not... nor consider' is softened in 65.17 by the use of passive
verbs: 'the former things shall not be remembered nor come to
mind'.

There is, however, more than a difference of style and
expression distinguishing 56.1 from 46.13. The context of the
two verses is not the same. In 46.13 the imminence of
Yahweh's action is affirmed in the face of stubborn refusal to
believe, whereas 56.1 is exhortatory in tone rather than con-
frontational, setting out the response required from the community by way of practical action which includes sabbath-
keeping. Here immediately in this concern with the sabbath
(cf. 58.13) is a significant difference from Second Isaiah
reflecting the changed situation of the postexilic period.

A similar subtle difference in tone becomes apparent when
62.11 is compared with 40.9-10. In place of the dramatic
proclamation of 40.9, 'Behold your God', Third Isaiah
announces, 'Behold, your salvation comes', employing an
abstract term as a designation of Yahweh such as we find in
liturgical contexts (cf. Ps. 27.1, and for a similarly abstract
designation of God see Ps. 144.2 RSV *margin*). The meaning is
defined more exactly, however, in what follows which seems
to have been taken verbatim from 40.10: 'his reward is with
him, and his recompense before him'. This makes it clear that
although the language may seem less direct, no other than
Yahweh himself is meant. This passage, too, is instructive as

an illustration of both continuity and discontinuity with
Second Isaiah. The latter clearly expects a sudden and dramatic intervention by God, an imminent deliverance of a
physical kind. Third Isaiah speaks rather of a transformation
of society. The difference in context should also be noted. In
Second Isaiah there follows the picture of a shepherd with his
flock on the move, symbolic of the imminent return from exile;
in Third Isaiah a reference to Jerusalem follows, as was
appropriate to a community resettled in its homeland and
longing for its capital city to be restored to its past glory as 'a
city not forsaken'. Third Isaiah may be said, therefore, to
soften to some extent the direct impact of Second Isaiah's
language.

Against this, however, must be set the fact that in some
instances Third Isaiah avoids certain ambiguities which occur
in Second Isaiah. Whereas the identity of the herald in 40.9-10
is unclear (is it Jerusalem herself or an unspecified messenger?), in 62.11 it is Yahweh himself who proclaims the coming
salvation. We may add that there is at least one passage
common to both which seems more appropriate to its context
in Third Isaiah than in Second Isaiah. In 60.4a (= 49.18a)
Israel is bidden, 'Lift up your eyes round about and see; they all
gather together, they come to you'. 'They', it is clear, are her
returning sons and daughters whom she will 'see and be radi-
ant' (v. 5). In contrast, the identical words in 49.18 have slight,
if any, connection with their context, a fact noted by a number
of commentators, and explained by Whybray on the grounds
that 'the images tumble over one another without regard for
logic'. We are, at any rate, warned against judging Third
Isaiah too harshly in contrast to his famous predecessor!

If Third Isaiah's style is sometimes less forceful than his
predecessor's so, too, expressions used by Second Isaiah in a
specific context are sometimes reapplied by Third Isaiah in a
more general fashion. 58.8 will serve as an illustration. Here
the expression 'the glory of the Lord shall be your rearguard'
is without doubt a reminiscence of 52.12, 'the God of Israel will
be your rearguard'. In Second Isaiah this is set clearly in the
context of a return from exile which is envisaged as a new
exodus and draws on the language of the exodus tradition. In

Third Isaiah, however, there is no such specific context. These words are now a general description of Israel's future blessedness. It seems justifiable, then, to conclude that Third Isaiah's use of language is here, at any rate, more abstract and general than his predecessor's. Yet once again a comparison of these two similar expressions, set as they are in different contexts, suggests some interesting observations. In place of Second Isaiah's reference to 'the God of Israel', Third Isaiah, somewhat after the manner of the priestly writer, prefers to speak of 'the glory of the Lord' (though cf. also 40.5), an attempt, perhaps, in his particular circumstances to safeguard the idea of Yahweh's transcendence. The exact significance of the preceding expression, 'your righteousness shall go before you', is not easy to determine. It is unclear whether this is intended as a parallel expression, and thus as a further designation of Yahweh (cf. Jer. 23.6) or whether it refers to the obligation of righteous action on the part of the people of God, similar to that with which Third Isaiah begins (56.1-2). If the second alternative is correct, it is an example of the distinctive ethical emphasis which pervades chs. 56–66. The transcendent God requires from his people the response of righteous action.

A further instance of the tendency in Third Isaiah to speak less directly of God is apparent in the comparison of 55.5 with 60.9. The two passages speak in almost identical terms (apart from the use respectively of masculine and feminine suffixes for Israel) of the source of Israel's glory as 'the Lord your God...the Holy One of Israel', but the preference in 60.9 for the expression 'the *name* of the Lord' is to be noted. Certainly the theme of God's transcendence appears prominently in Third Isaiah (see especially 57.15 and 66.1-2).

Moreover, it is arguable that the postexilic situation reflected in chs. 56–66 has produced a somewhat stronger emphasis than there is in 40–55 on the promise of glory for Israel—motivated, in all probability, by the urgent need for encouragement of the disheartened community. Whereas 44.23 and 49.3 speak unequivocally of glory accruing to Yahweh as a result of the restoration of his people, it is less clear from the form of the Hebrew that this is the meaning in 60.21 and 61.3. It is possible that what we have here is primarily a promise of glory for Israel, especially as the other occurrences of the verb 'to glorify' (*pā'ar*) in Third Isaiah (60.7, 13) refer to glorifying the temple, which is itself a prominent concern of these chapters which distinguishes them from Second Isaiah.

A passage of particular interest for its connection with, yet divergence from, Second Isaiah is 57.14: 'Build up, build up, prepare the way, remove every obstruction from my people's way'. This contains clear echoes of 40.3, but whereas the latter speaks in terms of a royal processional way, reflecting its exilic Babylonian background, in 57.14 the way which is to be prepared is a provision for the people. Nor is it any longer a question of a physical return to the homeland, but rather of the preparation of the community for its continued relationship with God: the word 'obstruction' (*mikšōl*) is used frequently in Ezekiel (7.19; 14.4, 7; 18.30 and 44.12) to refer to sin (cf. also Ps. 119.165). Here once more we find Third Isaiah's characteristic emphasis on ethical obligation. There is here both exhortation and encouragement: exhortation to attend to the spiritual life of the community, and encouragement to the dispirited in the assurance that the holy, transcendent God is pleased to dwell with the humble.

The relation to this passage of the similar summons in 62.10 is uncertain, for there the context is different and the metaphorical reference to the community's life is less clear. It may be that in this latter instance the prophet is urging upon the already resettled community the obligation to give a generous welcome to those yet to return from exile as Westermann suggests. Whybray, on the other hand, understands 'gates' to refer to the temple, and sees here an encouragement to the community to engage in worship. In short, despite the strong resemblance of 57.14 and 62.10 to Second Isaiah's summons in 40.3, and to his characteristic use of a double imperative (cf. 40.1; 52.1, 11), the whole tenor of the passages in Third Isaiah is different. Not only are they noticeably less dramatic in tone; they are also given fresh content. In place of Second Isaiah's description of the miraculous transformation of nature, we have in 62.12 the promised transformation of the community's relationship with God, and in 57.15 a great theological statement concerning the nature of God's dwelling among his people.

It is important that due weight should be given to the distinct changes in tone and expression, such as those discussed above, which mark so many of Third Isaiah's allusions to Second Isaiah; otherwise we fail to catch the subtle nuances of his message and so fail to appreciate his particular perspective. It is generally agreed by scholars that his original audience was familiar with Second Isaiah's message, and it is, therefore, a reasonable assumption that the element of surprise created by these unexpected echoes of familiar sayings in a different context and with a new twist to their meaning was a deliberate attempt to stimulate the attention of his hearers. For the modern reader, too, the recognition of a deliberate shift in the meaning or emphasis of an allusion not only increases the impact of the sayings concerned but in some particular instances helps us to see in perspective what might otherwise, for example, appear as excessive gloating over a defeated enemy. Why, for example, should 'the sons of those who oppressed you' (60.14) be specifically included among those who come to pay homage to God's people? The answer lies in recognizing here once again the motif of reversal, for three times in 51.18-20 Zion's loss of *her sons* at the hands of the enemy is stressed. Similarly, the expectation that 'all who despised you shall bow down at your feet' (60.14) deliberately picks up the taunting words of Jerusalem's oppressors, 'Bow down, that we may pass over' (51.23). A particularly striking echo of Second Isaiah occurs in 57.7. Here the expression 'a high mountain' (*har-gābōah*), which describes in 40.9 the place where Yahweh's advent as king is to be proclaimed, is applied ironically to the scene of Israel's apostasy.

The brief summons to Zion to 'arise, shine' (60.1) is to be set against the contrasting fate of that other female personification, 'the virgin daughter of Babylon', whose fall from royal splendour to servitude is graphically depicted in an extended metaphor (47.1-13). At Yahweh's advent Zion, the oppressed, is to be raised from humiliation to glory. The images of light and glory in this passage contrast powerfully with the terms for shame, silence and darkness in the other.

Both prophets alike are proclaiming God's power to reverse the status quo, but Second Isaiah is concerned with the fall of a tyrannical empire, whereas Third Isaiah addresses himself to the impoverished community centred on Jerusalem.

Does Third Isaiah Misunderstand Second Isaiah?

Commentators have sometimes suggested that Third Isaiah fails at times to understand correctly what he borrows from Second Isaiah. However, in the light of the deliberate shifts in context and meaning discussed above, this impression probably arises from a failure to recognize the subtle nuances of his reapplication of his predecessor's words. 60.13 has sometimes been quoted as a case in point. Here, in describing the materials used for beautifying the sanctuary, the prophet uses the same language as 41.19, where 'the cypress, the plane and the pine' are living trees whose growth is to transform the desert. But is it likely that anyone would misunderstand so obvious an allusion? Rather it is this very shift in meaning which gives impact to Third Isaiah's words, for this is a memorable affirmation that it is now not the desert which is to be transformed but devastated Jerusalem itself. The words are carefully chosen. This is poetic imagery. The trees 'shall *come*', that is, of their own accord, after the manner of the sacrificial animals (v. 7), not brought by foreign nations. This is not an example of a strange and inexplicable obtuseness on the part of the prophet but a new and significant slant given to a familiar saying. Similarly Westermann (following Duhm) raises the question whether the description of the prophet's role in 61.1, 'to proclaim good tidings', is based on a misunderstanding of 40.9 and 52.7 as a reference to Second Isaiah himself. This, too, is improbable, since in Third Isaiah's usage the verb (*bāśar*) is not restricted to prophetic activity but is used also of the proclamation of Yahweh's praise by those outside the Israelite community (see 60.6).

Since, as has already been indicated, there is evidence in chs. 56–66 of intentional, sometimes ironic, reinterpretation of earlier material, it is unlikely that the examples given above betray simple misunderstanding on the prophet's part. The not infrequent use of striking imagery in these chapters, the superb quality of much of the poetry and the careful artistry of the structure (see above pp. 18-20), together with the powerful challenge inherent in his words, all indicate that here is a prophet, who, while undoubtedly owing much to Second Isaiah and reapplying his words to a later situation, yet has a message to give which is distinctively his own. It is also a mistake to limit Third Isaiah's horizons too narrowly to the words of his predecessor. Chapters 56–66 show the influence not only of Second Isaiah but also of Israel's wider traditions, not least her liturgical worship and Wisdom writings. As was noted above, it may be due to the influence of the Psalms that God is referred to in abstract terms as 'your salvation' (62.11). The promise of 58.10-11 contains echoes of Job 11.17 and of Prov. 3.5-8, especially of v. 8, and the conclusion of the same chapter uses the terminology of Job 22.26 and Deut. 32.13. The evildoers in 59.7a are described in terms virtually identical to Prov. 1.16. Ezekiel's usage, it has already been noted, is reflected in the use of 'stumbling block' (*mikšōl*) in 57.14, and this is also true of the description of the sanctuary (*miqdās*; a term frequent in Ezekiel but never in Second Isaiah) as 'the place of my feet' (60.13; cf. Ezek. 43.7, 'the place of the soles of my feet'). Other examples could be multiplied, but these are sufficient warning against limiting the literary and theological influences on Third Isaiah's message simply to the tradition of Second Isaiah.

Further Reading

Details of works other than standard commentaries referred to in this chapter:

W.W. Cannon, 'Isaiah 61.1-3: an Ebed-Jahweh Poem', *ZAW* 47 (1929), pp. 284-88.

R.E. Clements, 'The Unity of the Book of Isaiah', in J.L. Mays and P.J. Achtemeier (eds.), *Interpreting the Prophets* (Philadelphia: Fortress Press, 1987).

L. Liebreich, 'The Compilation of the Book of Isaiah', *JQR* 46 (1955–56), pp. 259-77; *JQR* 47 (1956-57), pp. 114-38.

S. Mowinckel, *Jesaja-disiplene. Profeten fra Jesaja til Jeremia* (Oslo, Forlagt AV. H. Aschhoug [W. Nygaard], 1925).

J.F.A. Sawyer, 'Daughter of Zion and Servant of the Lord in Isaiah: A Comparison', *JSOT* 44 (1989), pp. 89-107.

C.R. Seitz, 'The One Isaiah//The Three Isaiahs', in C.R. Seitz (ed.) *Reading and Preaching the Book of Isaiah* (Philadelphia: Fortress Press, 1988), pp. 1-22.

M.A. Sweeney, *Isaiah 1–4 and the Post-Exilic Understanding of the Isaianic Tradition* (BZAW, 171; Berlin: de Gruyter, 1988).

On the continuity of the Isaianic tradition as due to the existence of a school of disciples see:

J.H. Eaton, 'The Origin of the Book of Isaiah', *VT* 9 (1959), pp. 138-57.

—'The Isaiah Tradition', in *Israel's Prophetic Tradition. Essays in Honour of Peter R. Ackroyd* (ed. R. Coggins, A. Phillips, M. Knibb; Cambridge: Cambridge University Press, 1982).

In addition to Torrey and Smart the following argue for the unity of Isaiah 40–66:

B.O. Banwell, 'A Suggested Analysis of Isaiah XL-LXVI', *ExpTim* 76 (1964–65).

L. Glahn, *Die Einheit von Kap. xl-lxvi des Buches Jesaja* (Giessen: Töpelmann, 1934).

E. König, *Das Buch Jesaja* (Gütersloh: Bertelsmann, 1926).

Special studies:

J. Blenkinsopp, 'Second Isaiah—Prophet of Universalism', *JSOT* 41 (1988), pp. 92-103 who describes Third Isaiah's relationship to Second Isaiah as that of commentary to text.

W.A.M. Beuken, 'The Main Theme of Trito-Isaiah "The Servants of Yahweh" ', *JSOT* 47 (1990), especially pp. 96-97.

W. Brueggemann, 'Unity and Dynamic in the Isaiah Tradition', *JSOT* 29 (1984), pp. 89-107, on the theological significance of the book of Isaiah as a whole.

K. Elliger, *Deuterojesaja in seinem Verhältnis zu Tritojesaja* (BWANT, 45; Stuttgart: Kohlhammer, 1928).

J.H. Steck, 'Tritojesaja im Jesajabuch', in J. Vermeylen (ed.) *Le Livre d'Isaïe: Les oracles et leurs relectures. Unité et complexité de l'ouvrage* (BETL, 81; Leuven: Leuven University Press, 1989), pp. 11-53.

J. Vermeylen, 'L'unité du livre d'Isaïe', in Vermeylen (ed.), *Le Livre d'Isaïe*, pp. 361-406.

W. Zimmerli, 'Zur Sprache Tritojesajas', in *Festschrift L. Köhler* (Bern, 1950), pp. 110-22 (= *Gottes Offenbarung. Gesammelte Aufsätze zum Alten Testament* [Theologische Bücherei, 19; Munich: Kaiser Verlag, 1963], pp. 217-33).

4

AUTHORSHIP AND DATE

THE QUESTIONS OF AUTHORSHIP and date are among the most difficult of the problems which confront us in the study of Isaiah 56–66. There is no unanimity among scholars on either question. Some argue for multiple authorship; others attribute the material in the main to a single author. Nor is there any greater agreement on the question of date. Opinions expressed vary between dating virtually all of the material, with few exceptions, to the early postexilic period (Whybray) and, on the other hand, regarding it in terms of a much longer time span extending from the pre-exilic period down to the third century BC (Volz). It should be noted that if the material does belong to the sixth or fifth centuries it constitutes the main evidence for the continuance of pre-exilic superstitious rituals and illegitimate forms of worship into the early post-exilic community.

A Single Author?

It was Duhm who first demonstrated that chs. 56–66 are of different authorship from 40–55. He attributed them to a single author who lived shortly before the time of Nehemiah in the mid-fifth century BC to whom he gave the name Trito-Isaiah. His general arguments for differentiating Third from Second Isaiah have been accepted by many scholars, although a few continue to defend the unity of authorship of chs. 40–66, rejecting the idea that it is in any way appropriate to speak of a Third Isaiah. Among those who argued for the unity of 40–

66 was C.C. Torrey, who held that chs. 40–66 as a whole,
together with 34–35, are to be attributed to a single author
who wrote about the year 400 BC. On this point he was categorical. To sustain his argument, however, he was compelled
to regard certain passages in Second Isaiah, including the
Cyrus passages, as later interpolations. In more recent years
J.D. Smart has similarly argued for the unity of authorship of
40–66. He differs from Torrey, however, on the question of
date, locating the material in a Palestinian setting a century
or so earlier towards the end of the exilic period. The arguments of neither of these scholars have proved generally convincing. Even among those who are in general agreement
with Duhm that chs. 56–66 are basically the work of a single
author who is not to be identified with Second Isaiah, there is a
wide difference of opinion on the question of date. The following examples illustrate the complexity of the problem.

Elliger argued on stylistic grounds that chs. 56–66 owe their
origin to a disciple of Second Isaiah who was also responsible
for collecting, and supplementing, the oracles in 40–55. He
regarded the material as contemporary with Haggai and
Zechariah—a time when the rebuilding of the temple was a
matter of pressing concern. Kessler, another advocate of
single authorship, is reluctant to give these chapters a more
precise date than the general period between the return from
exile in 538 and the mid-fifth century, the time of Nehemiah.
A more radical departure from Duhm's position is that proposed by McCullough, who challenges the general consensus
of opinion that the author of chs. 56–66 was *later* than Second
Isaiah, and that this prophet's role was to encourage a community despondent at the non-fulfilment of Second Isaiah's
promises. On the basis of two references which seem to imply
that the temple was not yet rebuilt (63.18; 64.10) McCullough
argues that Third Isaiah should be dated early in the exile,
between the years 587 and 562. Although it is probable that the
lament in 63.7–64.12 does belong to the beginning of the exile,
so early a date for Third Isaiah as a whole has not met with
general agreement.

Multiple Authorship

Scholarly opinion in general inclines to the view that the considerable diversity in content is sufficiently great to make the attribution of chs. 56–66 to a single author implausible. The stern denunciation of the community's leaders (56.9-12), the description of illicit religious practices rife within the community (57.1-13; 65.1-7), and the accusation that their religious observances are simply a matter of ritual without regard to social obligation (ch. 58) all stand awkwardly alongside the unconditional promises in chs. 60–62. It is difficult also to relate these promises, which are addressed to the entire community, to the situation of tension and outright opposition between hostile factions which is the background of 65.8-16 and 66.5.

It is readily apparent, too, that there are divergent, if not irreconcilable, attitudes towards some of the major issues with which these chapters are concerned. One of the most striking of these is the attitude shown towards Gentiles. The chapters begin and end with an open-hearted generosity towards foreigners which is unmatched by anything else in the Old Testament. These are invited, on fulfilment of certain conditions, to become full and equal members in the worshipping community with those of Jewish descent (56.3-8). Still more surprising is the final chapter where it is envisaged that some of foreign birth may share even in the service of the sanctuary as priests and Levites (66.18-21). The central chs. 60–62, however, display a different attitude towards foreigners. It is true that they are to have a share in the promised blessings, nations and their kings coming from the surrounding darkness to share in the radiance poured out on Zion (60.3). It must be said, however, that this is not primarily for their own sake. They hold a subordinate position as witnesses of Israel's glory. They are the agents, too, through whom the scattered exiles will be gathered home and the wealth of nations brought to Jerusalem (vv. 4-9)—wealth so abundant and safety so assured that the city's gates will stay open day and night (v. 11). It is foreigners who will rebuild Jerusalem's walls and their kings who will minister to her (v. 10). The passage is not vindictive or antagonistic. There is no gloating over the prospect that those who were Israel's oppressors will themselves be oppressed (contrast 45.14); they are nevertheless envisaged as coming to pay homage to those who were formerly their captives (v. 14). The tone is not polemical. This is not vengeance for vengeance's sake but evidence of the great reversal which God will work for his people (v. 14). Israel, whose wealth was torn from her at the time of deportation will, in a somewhat strange metaphor, 'suck the milk of nations and the breast of kings' (v. 16). Throughout ch. 60, with one exception, the picture is consistent: the nations are welcomed as witnesses of God's saving action and as participants in it, though their role is primarily as instruments of Israel's restoration, and only secondarily for their own blessing. The one discordant note in this chapter is the threat of ruthless annihilation for any nation which rejects this subordinate role (60.12). It is widely agreed, however, that both the form and the content of this verse indicate that it is intrusive here. Elsewhere in the chapter there is nothing to suggest that this role will not be undertaken willingly. The position of foreigners in ch. 61 is equally subordinate. It is native-born Israelites who are to be 'priests of the Lord', having their daily needs supplied by the work of aliens and foreigners (v. 6), just as Israel herself had traditionally supported the priesthood. They will testify also to Israel's vindication (61.9). With ch. 62 there is a slight though noticeable shift in perspective. Although the idea of the nations as witnesses of Israel's glory (62.2) is in line with chs. 60–61, they appear in v. 8 to be merely outsiders with no share in Israel's blessings. The thought here is simply one of reversal. The looting and pillage of the past will be ended. In the joyful setting of worship Israel will feast on what she herself has garnered—a rather different picture from 61.5.

Still more at variance with the generous attitude towards Gentiles shown in chs. 56 and 66 is the divine warrior passage in 63.3-6 where God is portrayed as trampling the nations to annihilation in the wine press of his anger, traditional symbol ism found also in Lam. 1.15, where it refers to judgment on Judah, and in Joel 3.13 (4.13).

Another point on which there are divergent strands within the material concerns the attitude taken to the importance of the Jerusalem temple. For the most part in these chapters its centrality in the community's life and worship is emphasized. It is in association with the temple that the full acceptance of eunuch and foreigner into the community's life is to be achieved. It is here that the former are guaranteed a future memorial 'better than sons and daughters' (56.5), and the latter a welcome into the joyful place of prayer (v. 7). Jerusalem's restoration is to include enrichment of the temple (60.7; cf. v. 13), and the bounty of secure harvests is to be celebrated 'in the courts of my sanctuary' (62.9). The centrality of the temple is symbolized, too, both in the description of Israel's role in the future age as 'priests of the Lord' (61.6), and in the characterization of illegitimate worship as forgetting 'my holy mountain' (65.11). It is from the temple, too, that the Lord's voice proclaims judgment (66.6). There are three passages, however, which focus, in contrast, not on the earthly temple but on heaven as Yahweh's dwelling place (though these are not, of course, mutually exclusive ideas as is clear from 1 Kgs 8.30). In the first of these passages God is said to inhabit eternity (57.15), and in this context 'my holy mountain' (v. 13) refers not to the Jerusalem temple but to the land of Israel, as the parallel expression indicates. In the second passage, namely the great lament of 63.7–64.12 where the temple appears to be in ruins (63.18; 64.11), God is entreated to look down from his heavenly dwelling (63.15), to rend the heavens and come to the help of his people (64.1). The problem arises chiefly with the third passage (66.1) which seems to imply outright opposition to the very idea of a restored earthly temple. Here heaven is described as God's throne and earth as his footstool (a striking contrast to 60.13 where it is the Jerusalem temple which is called 'the place of my feet'). Duhm's view that the opposition expressed here is directed against the schismatic Samaritan temple is difficult to sustain on chronological grounds, and it is now generally agreed that the Jerusalem temple is meant. Debate centres, however, on

whether this is to be understood as outright rejection of the
temple and of the sacrificial worship practised there (v. 3), or
whether it is an example of hyperbole, to be compared with
Hos. 6.6 and Ps. 50.8-13 on the question of sacrifice. In the
context of the Old Testament as a whole it is unlikely that we
have here the total repudiation of the earthly temple with its
system of sacrifices (v. 3); more probably this is an affirmation
of the priority of commitment over external rituals (cf. Ps.
50.14-15). If this is the intended meaning the passage does not
ultimately conflict with the importance attaching to the
Jerusalem temple elsewhere in these chapters, but rather
emphasizes the inadequacy of worship devoid of moral transformation. In this case it may be compared to the attitude
towards fasting in 58.6, where concern for the poor and
deprived clearly takes precedence over ritual even though the
practice of fasting in its traditional sense is probably not
excluded. In any case, 66.1-2 does not stand in isolation. The
connection in thought between 66.2 and 57.15 is clear even
though the Hebrew terms used for 'the humble and contrite'
are not the same. (For a summary of different interpretations
of 66.1 see Muilenburg.)

Finally, the fact that future hope, which generally in these
chapters is portrayed in this-worldly, even if idealistic (e.g.
65.18-23) terms, is in a few passages coloured by apocalyptic
overtones (60.19-20; 65.17; 66.22) strongly suggests both a
difference in origin and a later stage of development. In short,
it is difficult to maintain that the material has that kind of
inner consistency which would make it reasonable to attribute
it to a single author.

Date

The problems concerning authorship have involved us
already in the disputed question of the date of the material.
The possibility that it comes from different authors belonging
to different periods, together with the fact that the chapters
are singularly devoid of identifiable historical references,
compounds the problem. Taken as a whole it is clear that the
community was not in exile, but was concerned with regulat-

ing its religious life and worship in its homeland, with the temple at its centre (56.3-7; 58). There seems to be an expectation that other exiles would yet return (60.4-9, though 56.8, to judge from its context, seems to refer to Gentiles). The nature of the blessings promised in chs. 60–62 implies that the country was still impoverished as the result of devastation (62.4). There are memories of forced labour, of an enemy pillaging and looting (60.17-18). The general impression given is of a time soon after the return from exile when the community, depleted and demoralized, was endeavouring to reestablish itself and reaffirm its identity; but it is difficult to be entirely certain of this, for there were undoubtedly other periods of destruction following enemy attack (cf. Neh. 1.3). The many echoes of Second Isaiah in chs. 60–62, however, suggest in general a time not far removed from his. In a few instances, most prominently in 65.8-15 and 66.5, there are signs that the community was torn by factions. The cause of the dissension is not clear. One possibility is that it arose from conflict between the hopes and ideals of the returned exiles and those of the people who had remained throughout the time of the exile in Judah; for further discussion of this topic see Chapter 6.

One of the difficulties in the way of dating the material in chs. 56–66 lies in the incompleteness of our knowledge of the postexilic period. Apart from major events such as the return from exile under Cyrus in 538, the rebuilding of the temple between 520 and 515, and the general circumstances prevailing in the time of Nehemiah and Ezra (though here the chronology is fraught with particular difficulties), there is insufficient evidence available to give a clear picture of the history of postexilic Judah. Malachi provides some evidence of the sadly apathetic situation in Judah in the mid-fifth century, though here again there are a number of uncertainties.

When it comes to attempting to date individual passages, the sheer divergence of scholarly views indicates the ambiguity and uncertainty of the evidence. Volz considered that the material extends over a considerable period of time, from preexilic days (56.9-12) down to the Hellenistic period, the lower limit being indicated by the reference to Gad and Meni in

65.11. The worship of these two deities was not, however, confined to the Hellenistic period but had existed already at an earlier time. The lament of 63.7–64.12 is consistent with the early years of the exile, but probability is not the same as certainty and here, too, opinions differ. It is possible to argue that this lament belongs to the mid-fifth century, and reflects some of the disorders which marked the period of Nehemiah and Ezra. Although the enemies mentioned (63.18) are generally understood to be external enemies, we cannot be certain on this point. They may be enemies within the community who are misusing the sanctuary. This is just one example of the many exegetical problems which make it difficult to be certain of the historical background.

Relation to Haggai and Zechariah 1–8

There are several aspects of chs. 56–66 which make it probable that part at least of the material is contemporary with the prophets Haggai and Zechariah. The impoverished life of the community which is the background to Haggai (1.6, 8-11; 2.15-17) is not dissimilar to that which appears to underly the promises of chs. 60–62; and Haggai's vision of the treasures of the nations pouring into Jerusalem and filling Yahweh's house with splendour (2.7-9) expresses much the same hope as Isa. 60.5, 13. Similarly, Zechariah's promise that 'those who are far off shall come and help to build the temple of the Lord' (7.15) is not far removed from the expectation of Isa. 60.10. But whereas the efforts of Haggai and Zechariah to ensure the rebuilding of the temple are, on the internal evidence of the texts, to be dated in the year 520, their task having been accomplished by 515 BC, the historical situation of Third Isaiah is far less certain. There are two clear references to the temple lying in ruins (63.18; 64.11), but both occur within the same lament which, on the basis of its content, is generally attributed, as we have seen, to the early years of the exile, though whether it originated among the exiles or among those who remained in Judah—a community now recognized as of considerably more significance than had previously been thought—is uncertain. But, whatever the precise origin of the lament, its inclusion in this postexilic collection of oracles doubtless reflects its continuing use in worship even when the exile was over. In fact Westermann, as noted above, regards it as part of the penitential context in which the great promises of chs. 60–62 were delivered.

Elsewhere in Third Isaiah, apart from 65.11 where it is not clear whether or not the temple is in ruins, its existence as a place of worship seems to be presupposed (56.5, 7; 62.9; 66.6, 20), although it lacks the splendour of earlier times (60.7, 13; cf. Hag. 2.3); consequently a date after 515 would be required. The problems surrounding the meaning of 66.1 have already been briefly discused under 'authorship', and the possibility that that verse is not an outright rejection of the temple but rather an example of hyperbole has been mentioned. It is conceivable, however, that it does express opposition to Haggai's emphasis on the priority for the community's well-being of the restoration of the temple (Hag. 1.9). If this is so it must belong to the period prior to 515 if not to 520 BC.

There is a further interesting connection between Third Isaiah and Zechariah in that both prophets find themselves in a situation where the question of fasting needs to be addressed (Isa. 58; Zech. 7.3; 8.19). The issue which Zechariah faces concerns the appropriateness of observing the customary fast days now that the exile is over. His response to the question is to reiterate the primary obligation of social justice. The precise situation to which Isaiah 58 belongs is less clear, but this prophet, too, like Zechariah, is concerned not to impose negative restrictions on the community but to affirm the positive obligation to provide for the disadvantaged, the hungry and the homeless. The passage in Zechariah concludes by looking back to the past, to the reason for God's judgment on his people in the experience of exile: '"As I called, and they would not hear, so they called, and I would not hear", says the Lord of hosts' (7.13). Isa. 58.9, in contrast, looks to the future, in terms which appear to be a deliberate reversal of Zechariah's words of judgment: 'then [i.e. when the needs of the poor are supplied] you shall call, and the Lord will answer; you shall cry, and he will say, Here I am'. The implications of this for the date of the Isaiah passage cannot, however, be pressed beyond the fact that it suggests an acquaintance with Zechariah's words.

Relation to the Work of Nehemiah

Despite the apparent connections with the words and work of Haggai and Zechariah, there are several aspects of Isaiah 56–66 which may suggest a link rather with the time of Nehemiah in the mid-fifth century, the date favoured by Duhm. Once again, however, it has to be admitted that the evidence is ambivalent and inconclusive. This later period might seem more appropriate to the references to the 'ancient ruins...the devastations of many generations' (61.4; cf. 58.12); yet even by the first generation after the exile the destruction of 587 could be so described, especially when, as here, the language is poetic (Whybray). The desirability of an increase in population was felt in many periods of Israel's history, and there is no need to assume a connection between the background to the promise of progeny in 60.22 and Nehemiah's task of repopulating Jerusalem (11.1). It must be remembered that from early times this was a fundamental aspect of the ancient patriarchal promises in Genesis.

As regards the welcome given to foreigners to share in the worshipping community (56.3, 6-7), Blenkinsopp suggests two possible alternatives; either this attitude may have been motivated by opposition to Nehemiah's exclusive attitude towards those not of Israelite stock, or it may itself have been the reason for those restrictive measures. The situation envisaged here differs, however, in an important respect from that addressed by Nehemiah. The foreigners in question in Isaiah 56 are individual proselytes (cf. 44.5) threatened with exclusion from the community, possibly in the early years after the return from exile (cf. Ezra 4.1-3). In contrast, those excluded by Nehemiah were not adherents of the Jewish faith.

Three further aspects of the Isaiah material have sometimes been regarded as possibly connecting it with the time of Nehemiah. The first is the emphasis on building: the verb employed occurs more frequently in these chapters than in any other part of the Old Testament. This is not, of course, decisive evidence of such a date; we need to be reminded that there was destruction which needed urgent rebuilding at a period considerably later than the early years after the exile (Neh. 1.3). However, the hoped-for rebuilding of the city walls in which foreigners are to participate in 60.10 can hardly be connected with Nehemiah and his resistance to such outside assistance! Secondly, the emphasis in Third Isaiah on the importance of strict observance of the sabbath as a distinguishing mark of the community (56.2, 4, 6; 58.13) is reminiscent of Nehemiah's similar concern to reinstate this regulation (13.15-22). A third possible common element is the stress on the liberation of those deprived of freedom, for the prophet's commission, according to 61.1, is 'to proclaim liberty to the captives, and the opening of the prison to those who are bound'. This has been compared with Nehemiah 5. But the question remains, is it intended in a literal or in a metaphorical sense? Here we encounter one of the difficulties in the way of relating these chapters with confidence to the activities and concerns of Nehemiah: this may be a purely metaphorical expression describing the deliverance of the exiles, and thus closely similar to what is said about the role of the servant in Second Isaiah (49.9). On the other hand, one cannot exclude the possibility that the verse is meant to refer in a more literal way to those imprisoned, possibly for debt, a situation which certainly existed in Nehemiah's time and was among the social evils which blighted the community's life in the mid-fifth century, inflicted not by foreign enemies but through injustices perpetrated within the Jewish community itself. Certainly ch. 58 in its concern over the oppression of workers (v. 3) and the deprivation of the downtrodden, hungry, homeless and naked (vv. 6-7) reflects a situation not unlike that represented in Nehemiah 5.

Westermann's Theory of the Compilation of the Material

It was noted above in Chapter 2 that, speaking generally, Isaiah 56–66 has the form of a series of concentric circles around a central core consisting of chs. 60–62. Since it is within these central chapters that the most numerous reminiscences of Second Isaiah occur it is not unreasonable to suppose that they are close in time to the latter, whereas the situation envisaged in other passages, for example in the framework provided by chs. 56 and 66, appears to belong to a somewhat later date. An important discussion of the structure and formation of chs. 56–66 is to be found in the commentary by Westermann in which he outlines four main stages of development. He takes as his starting point chs. 60–62 which are widely agreed to form the nucleus of Third Isaiah. These three chapters form a literary unit with a common theme in that they consist of unqualified promises of salvation. It is clear from their content that they belong to the postexilic period, and their many links with Second Isaiah suggest that they originated from a follower or disciple of his. Three other passages (57.14-20; 65.16b-25; 66.6-14) also consist solely of promises of salvation and have close links with Second Isaiah, and on these grounds Westermann holds that they also belong to the core of Third Isaiah's message, though they were probably transmitted separately from 60–62. This central core itself may not be entirely free from traces of later development, particularly in the apocalyptic overtones of those passages where salvation is portrayed in supra-historical terms (60.19-20; 65.17, 25) but Westermann does not totally exclude the possibility that even these are part of Third Isaiah's own proclamation, though they are certainly not characteristic of it.

With these salvation oracles Westermann tentatively associates the conditional promises of 58.1-12, where also there are reminiscences of chs. 60–62, although he admits that this chapter shows signs of considerable development. In all of these passages the whole community is addressed. The central core of salvation oracles in 60–62 is preceded and followed by communal laments (59.1-15; 63.7–64.12). Westermann, as noted already, regards this arrangement whereby the promise of salvation is closely associated with lament as not simply the result of editorial activity but as a significant pointer to the context of repentance in which the promises of salvation were first pronounced. The lament in 63.7–64.12 he dates in the early exilic period.

Chapter 59 is altogether more complex in form (see Chapter 2). On the grounds that it includes not only lament but accusation against transgressors (vv. 3-8) Westermann suggests that it functions here as a connecting link between the central promises of salvation and the three prophetic oracles of judgment which precede them in 56.9-12, 57.3-6 and 57.7-13a, all of which he regards as pre-exilic in origin but reapplied here to the postexilic community. The framework within which 57.3-6 and 7-13a are set, namely vv. 1-2 and 13b, gives a hint of serious division within the community. Righteous and wicked are contrasted, as also is the destiny awaiting them, and the nation is no longer addressed as a whole. This divergence appears even more emphatically in 65.8-16a with its sharp contrast between Yahweh's servants and 'you', the evildoers who are directly addressed, and in this it is distinct from the utterances of the pre-exilic prophets. The evils of which this group are accused are purely cultic, and there is little relation to what Westermann sees as the original message of Third Isaiah. To this second stage in the formation of the tradition he assigns 66.5 and 17 also, which likewise reflect a situation of internal conflict.

A third and later strand, according to Westermann's analysis, is to be found in the judgment envisaged against foreign nations (63.1-6; 66.6, 15-16, 24). These passages occur only within the second major transmission complex and not within chs. 56–59, and they contrast strongly with Third Isaiah's own attitude to foreign nations. As remarked above, these are depicted in chs. 60–62 as sharing in the blessings promised to Israel, even though in a subordinate capacity. In Westermann's third strand, however, the judgment against the nations is harsh. Westermann attributes this element to a deliberate attempt to correct the attitude of 60–62 at a time when judgment against the nations had become axiomatic. Indeed, the harshest of these passages (63.1-6) is attached directly to chs. 60–62. Couched in the language of myth and having certain apocalyptic features, it portrays the final destruction of the nations, expressing an attitude similar to that of 60.12 which Westermann, with other commentators, regards as a later addition in its context. This same development is apparent also in ch. 66, where 66.7-14, which is itself part of the message of Third Isaiah, has been set within a framework of an 'epiphany of judgment' consisting of 66.6 and 15-16. 66.24, the final verse of the book of Isaiah, goes even further in this direction in speaking not only of the destruction of God's enemies but in describing this as 'eternal'. This condemnatory strand occurs only in the complex consisting of chs. 60–66, and this is also true of apocalyptic additions to the oracles of salvation, in which there is reference to new heavens and a new earth (60.19-20; 65.17, 25; 66.20, 22). Westermann considers that these also belong to the third stage of development.

To the fourth and final stage Westermann, like many other commentators, attributes the remarkable passages in 56.1-8 and 66.18-19, 21 where foreigners are admitted to the covenant community on equal terms with native-born Jews. With this generous attitude towards foreigners belongs also the emphasis on sabbath-keeping (56.2, 4, 6; 58.13). The facts that 56–58 begins and ends with emphasis on the sabbath and that 60–66 contains elements not found in 56–58 lead Westermann to the conclusion that the material existed originally in two separate complexes of tradition which were eventually brought together by those responsible for the fourth stage in development, giving Third Isaiah the form it has today.

Westermann's careful distinguishing of the various strands which create diversity in the material is a valuable contribution to discussion, although his approach is too schematized to prove entirely convincing. The history of the period is still too obscure for the precise development of the text to be traced with any certainty, and it is probable that the process was still more complex than Westermann's hypothesis suggests, for even the central core of the material shows evidence of considerable development. Hanson is justified in his criticism that Westermann's scheme is over-rigid, and that in consequence 'the entity Third Isaiah becomes absolutely static'. As circumstances changed, the form in which the community expressed its hopes inevitably changed. Hence Hanson seeks to direct attention instead to the sociological matrix which gave rise to the literature (on this see further Chapter 6), arguing that the futile search for an author thus becomes unnecessary, as does the continual reduction of the material into ever smaller units. He concludes that at the heart of the inner community struggle attested by these chapters lies a conflict between those who saw the future in apocalyptic terms and those who wished to preserve the status quo. As regards the date of the material, he concludes that it extends in the main from a time shortly after Second Isaiah down to the end of the sixth century BC, the whole having been gathered eventually into a collection between the years 475 and 425, to which period he attributes the redactional framework comprising 56.1-8 and 66.17-24. A fuller discussion of Hanson's approach and an evaluation of his conclusions will be found in Chapter 6.

Conclusion

The above discussion has shown how difficult it is to date the material with any precision. The different viewpoints expressed in the material suggest that it may cover a considerable period of time. In some instances the resemblance in tone to the accusations made by pre-exilic prophets makes an early date a possibility. The portrayal of Israel as a harlot has similarities to Ezekiel and may belong to the time before the fall of Jerusalem in 587. The indictment of inadequate leadership in 56.9-12 and the portrayal of idolatry in 57.7-13 are not out of keeping with the message of those earlier prophets. Yet to attribute these passages to pre-exilic prophets on the grounds that later prophecy had lost much of its force is an unwarrantable assumption. There is powerful poetry and vivid imagery in these chapters which add greatly to the impact of the message. But whether the passages in question were adopted from an earlier time or not, it is clear that abuses such as those referred to here existed in the postexilic community, and the challenge of the prophetic word needed to be brought to bear on them. At the other end of the time scale the indictment of idolatry in 65.3-5 and the reference to the cult of Gad (Fortune) and Meni (Destiny, v. 11) are generally regarded as postexilic, even Hellenistic, by some commentators, though it has to be admitted that the origin of these cults is of uncertain date. The fact that this same chapter is permeated by evidence of factions within the community suggests a postexilic date, but how early in that period this dissension showed itself is difficult to determine, though it is plausible to suggest that it arose from conflicts of interest and ideals probably soon after the return of the first of the exiles. The one fact that emerges clearly is the need for caution in attempting to date the material within any but broad limits.

Further Reading

Details of works referred to above:

J. Blenkinsopp, 'Second Isaiah—Prophet of Universalism', *JSOT* 49 (1988), p. 97.

K. Elliger, *Die Einheit des Tritojesajas* (BWANT, 45; Stuttgart: Kohlhammer, 1928). For criticism of his argument see Volz, *Jesaja II*, pp. 197ff. and P.D. Hanson, *The Dawn of Apocalyptic*, p. 36.

W. Kessler, 'Studien zur religiösen Situation im ersten nachexilischen Jahrhundert und zur Auslegung von Jes 56–66', *Wissenschaftliche Zeitschrift* 6 (1956-57), pp. 41-74.

W.S. McCullough, 'A Re-examination of Isaiah lvi-lxvi', *JBL* 67 (1948), pp. 27-36.

Muilenburg, *Isaiah Chapters 40–66*, pp. 757-60.

Westermann, *Isaiah 40–66*, pp. 296-308.

The following commentaries support the view that these chapters are in the main the work of a single author:

D.R. Jones (*Isaiah 56–66 and Joel*) regards Third Isaiah as basically the work of one man, dating the material between 538 and 520, with the exception of 56.1-8 which belongs after 515.

G.A.F. Knight (*The New Israel*) argues that the material was completed, probably with the help of disciples, before 525 BC.

J.J. Scullion, *Isaiah 40–66* (Old Testament Message, A Biblical-Theological Commentary, 12; Wilmington, DE: Michael Glazier/ Dublin: Gill & Macmillan, 1982).

The arguments in favour of multiple authorship are clearly set out in the commentaries by Westermann and Whybray. In addition the following may be consulted:

K. Budde, *Das Buch Jesaja, Kap. 40–66* (Tubingen, 1922).

G. Fohrer, *Das Buch Jesaja III* (Zurich: Zwingli, 1964).

P.D. Hanson, *The Dawn of Apocalyptic* (Philadelphia: Fortress Press, 1975).

H.G. Jefferson, 'Notes on the Authorship of Isaiah lxv and lxvi', *JBL* 68 (1949), pp. 225-30, who argues on stylistic grounds that these two chapters belong neither to Second nor to Third Isaiah but are the product of several other writers.

D. Michel, 'Zur Eigenart Tritojesajas', *Theologia Viatorum* 10 (1966), pp. 220-25.

5

THE ROLE OF PROPHET
AS REPRESENTED IN
THIRD ISAIAH

MY CONCERN IN THIS CHAPTER is neither to attempt to trace a single historical figure behind the text nor to discuss to what extent the oracles are the *ipsissima verba* of any particular prophet, but rather to discuss the presentation of the prophetic role. The material is too disparate, and its origins too obscure, to justify the historical approach. It is ultimately its final literary form which must concern us. It is clear that from start to finish these chapters are presented as a prophetic message. They begin with a standard prophetic formula, 'thus says the Lord' (56.1), signifying that the words which follow, expressed in the first person, are a divine message transmitted by the prophet as messenger. This is balanced by a similar formula which concludes the penultimate verse of the entire book (66.23). Similar expressions, with slight variations, occur at various points throughout the chapters as introductory or concluding formulas, most frequently—though not exclusively—in chs. 56 and 65–66: 'thus says the Lord' (56.4; 65.8, 13; 66.1, 12) or 'says the Lord/your God' (59.21; 65.7, 25; 66.9), and 'oracle of the Lord' (*ne'ūm YHWH* 56.8; 66.2, 17, 22). It is, then a legitimate question to ask how the role of prophet is portrayed in Isaiah 56–66.

The prophetic books of the Old Testament are not in any sense intended as biographies. The message, not the man, is the focus of attention, and reference to the prophet's life is included only in so far as it relates to the word by which God

challenges his people. This is well illustrated by the book of
Hosea. In popular thinking, questions about Hosea's personal
experience and marital problems often take pride of place; yet
in fact, even in chs. 1–3, where the experiences of the prophet
are brought into direct relationship with God's dealings with
Israel, there is no attempt to fill out the details of his personal
story. This is particularly evident in ch. 3 where, although
certain aspects of the prophet's experience are briefly elabo-
rated in illustration of Yahweh's dealings with his people, the
prophet's story is not completed but ends abruptly (3.3). Once
it has served its purpose as illustrating the divine activity it is
deliberately abandoned so that attention may be directed solely
to the prophet's primary concern, Israel's relationship with
God.

Yet even allowing for this general lack of interest in biogra-
phy as such, there is a marked contrast between the book of
Isaiah and the other two major collections of prophetic material, Jeremiah and Ezekiel, in both of which the person of the
prophet is given a certain prominence: the call-experience
appears in each case in ch. 1, and in Ezekiel is extended as far
as 3.11. In the book of Isaiah, however, the figure of the
prophet is only rarely perceived. It is in ch. 6 that we first
encounter the prophet, and only at this point do we learn of his
visionary experience culminating in his call to the prophetic
role. The contrast with the presentation of the prophet in
Jeremiah is particularly illuminating. The book of Jeremiah
shows signs of a complex process of development in the course
of which the persona of the prophet also seems to have under-
gone considerable development, with the result that it is possible to argue that 'perhaps the figure of Jeremiah is more the
creation of the tradition than the creator of it' (Carroll). In
Isaiah 1–39, however, the prophet appears only briefly; in his
call (ch. 6), in encounter with Ahaz (chs. 7–8), and in relation
to Hezekiah (chs. 37–39). In Second Isaiah the figure of the
prophet is almost totally retracted. It is generally agreed that
he appears briefly in 40.6 where he responds to the summons
to proclaim the good news: 'and I said, What shall I cry?',
though even here the Masoretic text is less specific, vocalizing
the Hebrew as 'and one said, what shall I cry?' If the person of

the prophet is apparent anywhere else in Second Isaiah it may be in the guise of the enigmatic figure of the servant in the Servant Songs, an identification accepted nowadays by an increasing number of scholars (cf. Whybray, *The Second Isaiah*). Consequently it comes as no surprise to find that the figure of the prophet is elusive also in chs. 56–66. The two main actors in the drama are Yahweh and Zion personified (Seitz). It is nevertheless useful to examine how the role of prophet is envisaged in this section of the Isaiah tradition.

A Prophet Addressed?

I shall begin by considering two passages (58.1; 59.21) where God addresses an unnamed individual—though it should be noted that these passages have little else in common with each other.

1. *Isaiah 58.1*
It is reasonable to assume that the individual addressed here is a prophetic figure summoned to the traditional prophetic task of proclaiming judgment on God's people:

> Cry aloud, spare not,
>> lift up your voice like a trumpet;
> declare to my people their transgression,
>> to the house of Jacob their sins (cf. Hos. 8.1; Mic. 3.8).

The figurative reference to the trumpet is particularly appropriate in this context concerned with the question of fasting, for the blowing of trumpets traditionally announced the observance of a fast (cf. Joel 2.15). The prophet may have been addressing the community during a period of fasting (Volz, Westermann). Interwoven with this proclamation of judgment on the community there is evidence of another prophetic role, for the traditional form of judgment oracle passes into the milder tones of exhortation with conditional promises of blessing in place of the expected pronouncement of punishment. The prophet is seen here in a different role, as one who is consulted by the people in their dilemma concerning the inefficacy of their careful ritual observance—a function which may be compared with 56.3-7 where a ruling (*torah*), in the guise of a prophetic word, is given on the qualifications necessary for admission to worship.

2. *Isaiah 59.21*

The second passage in which an anonymous figure is addressed by Yahweh is to be found in 59.21. Here it is less easy to determine the identity of the person so addressed. The passage seems to have no connection with its present context either in content or in style, for it is prose in the midst of poetry. Its juxtaposition with vv. 19-20 is best explained as due to the external link of a catchword (on which see above p. 16). The reference to 'spirit' (cf. 61.1) and 'words' (cf. 51.16) suggests that here too, as in 58.1, a prophetic figure is in mind. The matter is not, however, quite as simple to resolve as this identification would suggest, for the prophetic office in ancient Israel, unlike the priesthood, was not hereditary, and it must, therefore, be asked in what sense the promise, given in perpetuity, can be meant:

> My spirit which is upon you, and my words which I have put in your mouth, shall not depart out of your mouth, or out of the mouth of your children, or out of the mouth of your children's children, says the Lord, from this time forth and for evermore.

The words have something of a Deuteronomic ring about them, although even this needs to be qualified, for, as Whybray points out, the form of expression, 'as for me, this is my covenant with them', is more reminiscent of the priestly strand of the Pentateuch. His proposal that the reference here is not to an individual prophet but to prophecy as a gift for all God's people (cf. Joel 2.28-29) resolves to some extent the problem raised by the mention of future generations. Support for this view can be found in 51.16 where the statement, 'I have put my words in your mouth' seems, in view of the context, to refer to Zion personified rather than to an individual (so Muilenburg, who compares 44.3). We have here a statement of considerable importance for the eschatological perspective of these chapters. It is a filling out of the promise of

v. 20, a reversal by divine initiative of the despair portrayed in the lament earlier in the chapter with its emphasis not only on violent deeds but on lying words (vv. 3b-4, 13; cf. also v. 11). In either case, whether it refers to an individual prophet or to the community as a whole, it is an affirmation of the importance of Yahweh's word and spirit for the future of his people.

A Prophet Speaks?

There are in addition several instances in Isaiah 56–66 where the first-person form is used, suggesting that the speaker may be a prophetic figure. In contrast to the two references discussed above, these occur only in chs. 60–66, a fact which may add further support to Westermann's theory that two originally separate complexes of material have been brought together. In two instances (61.10; 63.7) it is likely that a prophet is speaking on behalf of the community, in thanksgiving and in the prelude to a lament respectively. As the lament progresses (63.7–64.12) the prophet is seen in his role as intercessor on the community's behalf. The other first-person references (61.1-3; 62.1, 6) are more ambiguous and are discussed below.

1. *Isaiah 61.1-3*
Some scholars, in view of its similarity in expression to 42.1, 7 and 49.8-9 see in this passage further reference to the servant figure of Second Isaiah. This allows not only for reference to an individual, whether prophet or otherwise, but also for a collective meaning, whether relating to Israel (Smart, Hanson) or to the Davidic dynasty as J.H. Eaton argues, citing in evidence the association of kingly anointing with endowment of the spirit in 1 Sam. 16.13 and 2 Sam. 23.2. It is arguable, however, that a prophet is the speaker here, affirming his consciousness of divine commissioning and describing the role to which he is committed; for although it is unusual to speak of the anointing of a prophet—a term usually applied to kings or, in the postexilic period, to priests—this is not unparalleled (cf. the probably metaphorical use of the term in 1 Kgs 19.16). Whether the reference to the liberation of captives in 61.1 is

meant in a literal or in a figurative sense is unclear (see above p. 63), but in either case the prophet's role is seen to be concerned with the restoration of well-being for the community, and the resultant manifestation of the Lord's glory (v. 3).

The sense of conviction of a personal call which comes across in these verses is no less authentic than in the case of earlier prophets such as Amos and First Isaiah. This is not diminished by the fact that, as Whybray comments, the prophet is to be seen as the interpreter of an old message rather than the bearer of a new one. The situation to which the message is addressed and the particular question of the delay in fulfilment of Second Isaiah's promises in spite of the return from exile give to his message a different character from that of his predecessors, yet his consciousness of being the spokesman of the divine word to God's people is no less real. 'To the best of our knowledge, this was the last occasion in the history of Israel on which a prophet expressed his certainty of having been sent by God with a message to his nation with such freedom and conviction' (Westermann).

The two remaining passages (62.1, 6) where the first-person form suggests that a prophet may perhaps be the speaker are unfortunately beset by difficult problems of interpretation. It is not clear either in 62.1 and or in 62.6 whether we have divine or prophetic speech—that is to say, whether the prophet is speaking on his own account or as Yahweh's spokesman (Jeremiah 4.19-22 is an instance of a similar ambiguity). We must in any case avoid assuming too readily that the speaker in the two verses is identical.

2. *Isaiah 62.1*

Most commentators hold that a prophet is the speaker here and that it is the traditional role of prophet as intercessor on the community's behalf that is emphasized (Volz, Westermann, Muilenburg). On this view the prophet is affirming his commitment to unremitting prayer on Zion's behalf until the time when she is openly vindicated before the Gentile nations by God's saving intervention. Intercession was indeed a primary aspect of a prophet's task (cf. Gen. 20.7), and the fact that Yahweh is referred to elsewhere in this context (vv. 2-5) in the third person supports this interpretation of the passage. Volz sees here a parallel with the singer in Psalm 137 who cannot forget Jerusalem.

These arguments are not, however, conclusive; and the alternative view that Yahweh is the speaker (Whybray) must not be dismissed too lightly. The verbs 'to keep silent' (*ḥāšāh*) and 'to rest' (*šāqat*) occur a number of times with Yahweh as subject (*ḥāšāh* in 57.11; 64.12; 65.6; cf. 42.14; Ps. 28.1; *šāqat* in Ps. 83.1 [MT 2]), though not exclusively so (cf. v. 6). On these grounds it can plausibly be argued that 62.1 is God's response to the community's lament in 63.1–64.12 which ends with the plea, 'Wilt thou restrain thyself at these things, O Lord? Wilt thou keep silent (*ḥāšāh*) and afflict us sorely?' Although Westermann recognizes the close connection between the lament and the promise of salvation, he prefers to understand v. 1 as a description of the prophet's role: 'he had been sent to counter God's silence and restraining of himself of which the state of things gave evidence... by loud proclamation of his promises', a situation to which he sees a parallel in Zech. 1.12.

3. *Isaiah 62.6-7*
Here again commentators are divided on the question whether this is the divine or the prophetic 'I'. The problem is compounded by the fact that Yahweh is referred to in the third person in vv. 6b-8a. Yet in what sense can a prophet be said to appoint 'watchmen' (*šōmᵉrīm*) over Jerusalem? If the term applies to prophets, the summons to this task is beyond question Yahweh's prerogative alone. Yet this argument is not as conclusive as it may at first appear, as comparison with Isa. 21.6 indicates, for there the prophet is commanded (no doubt in a figurative sense) to 'set a watchman' (*mᵉṣappeh*). Though the term used there for watchman is not the same as the usage in 62.6, the difference is hardly significant. In v. 6b the speaker is surely the prophet who urges unremitting intercession until God's promises to Jerusalem (v. 8) are fulfilled. Some of the awkwardness of v. 6a may be eased if we follow Whybray in preferring the meaning 'concerning (the building of) your walls' rather than 'upon your walls', which the

Hebrew expression is equally capable of bearing.

A further question remains. Up to this point we have assumed that the watchmen are to be identified as prophets whose task it is to intercede incessantly on Jerusalem's behalf. It is possible, however, that the 'remembrancers' (*mazkīrīm*) of the following verse, with whom the watchmen are probably to be identified, are angelic beings, a suggestion made by Whybray, though he himself regards the reference to prophets as more likely on the grounds that intercession was primarily a prophetic function. Muilenburg takes the speaker in v. 6a to be the Lord who appoints prophets to intercede for Jerusalem, and in v. 6b as the prophet who addresses the prophetic group of v. 6a as the Lord's *mazkīrīm*, a term used to denote a court official (2 Sam. 8.16; Isa. 36.3; cf. Esth. 6.1) whose duty it was to remind the monarch of his commitments.

To conclude: despite the problems of interpretation, we have in these chapters evidence of the continuation of traditional prophetic roles. The prophet intercedes on behalf of the community and is spokesman of the divine word in both judgment and salvation, although the former shades into the more muted tones of exhortation, culminating not in the pronouncement of punishment but in conditional promises of salvation. The prophet acts also as spokesman for the community in its worship, leading both lament and thanksgiving. Prophetic activity is still motivated by a sense of personal divine commissioning. Finally, if my understanding of 59.21 is correct, the prophetic vocation continues to be held in high regard, and the promise of participation in God's word and spirit is held out to all the faithful.

Further Reading

Works other than standard commentaries referred to above:

R.P. Carroll, *Jeremiah* (Old Testament Guides; Sheffield: JSOT Press, 1989).

J.H. Eaton, *Festal Drama in Deutero-Isaiah* (London: SPCK, 1979), pp. 90-91.

R.N. Whybray, *The Second Isaiah* (Old Testament Guides; Sheffield: JSOT Press, 1983).

C.R. Seitz, 'Isaiah 1–66. Making Sense of the Whole', in C.R. Seitz (ed.), *Reading and Preaching the Book of Isaiah* (Philadelphia: Fortress Press, 1988).

Other works:
W.A.M. Beuken, 'Servant and Herald of Good Tidings. Isaiah Ch. 61 as an Interpretation of Isaiah Ch. 40–55', in J. Vermeylen (ed.), *Le Livre d'Isaïe. Les oracles et leurs relectures. Unité et complexité de l'ouvrage* (Leuven: Leuven University Press, 1989), pp. 411-42.

W.W. Cannon, 'Isaiah 61.1-3: an Ebed-Jahweh Poem', *ZAW* 47 (1929), pp. 284-88.

6

PROBLEMS OF THE
POSTEXILIC COMMUNITY

SOME ASPECTS OF JEWISH SOCIETY in the postexilic period
have been included already in Chapter 4 in the discussion
about the date of the material. In the present chapter I shall
consider the specific question of the nature and causes of the
dissension which threatened to disrupt the life of the community in the period after the return from exile. In this
respect Isaiah 56–66 is of particular importance since it provides the main source of evidence for these internal divisions,
most clearly and unambiguously in 65.8-16 and 66.5, and also
in the framework to ch. 57 which consists of vv. 1-2 (the
meaning of v. 2 is very obscure) and 19-21, and possibly elsewhere if Hanson's thesis is accepted (on this see below). Even
in Second Isaiah, however, the beginnings of serious division
can be detected, and there are hints that already all was not
well in the community's life. There were some for whom
words of judgment were more appropriate than promises of
salvation. The following will serve as examples. At the end of
ch. 48 we have an oddly detached saying, '"There is no peace",
says the Lord, "for the wicked"' (cf. 57.21). Although, as is
probable, this is to be regarded as a later addition in its present
context, it is clear that there were some within the covenant
community who were deemed to 'confess the God of Israel, but
not in truth or right' (48.1). The fact that the situation was
evidently such as to elicit the severe warning in 50.11, 'This
shall you have from my hand: you shall lie down in torment',
is also some indication of the prevailing circumstances. It

seems a fair deduction, therefore, that some of the community's problems which are unmistakable in Third Isaiah were beginning to appear already during Second Isaiah's ministry. It is also not without significance that in Second Isaiah we have the beginnings of the transition from the designation of Israel as 'servant', which is so prominent a feature of chs. 40–55, to the plural 'servants' (54.17), used in Third Isaiah to signify the faithful within the community (65.8-9, 13-15). Even on a fairly superficial reading of Third Isaiah it is possible to detect some growth in the hostility existing between opposing factions (a process which Hanson feels able to trace in considerable detail on the basis of his own particular interpretation of the sociological background of the material). Whereas in 66.5 the rival group is described as 'your brethren', the polemical tone in 65.8-15 has become far more bitter. Here the very existence of the community seems threatened by the rival factions, and the exigencies of the situation have created a new literary genre. As noted in Chapter 2, this passage departs from the traditional prophetic form of distinct judgment and salvation oracles and brings the two into close relation with each other, addressing the opposing factions simultaneously, the one with threats of judgment, the other with promises of salvation.

When, however, we attempt to identify these opposing factions and to understand the issues which threatened to divide postexilic Judaean society we are faced with many uncertainties. The evidence is incomplete and often ambiguous—a warning against too readily constructing a hypothesis on insecure foundations. One commonly held opinion suggests that the roots of the problem lay in a conflict of interests, together with a divergence in theological orientation, between those who had remained in the land during the period of the exile and those who, through having been deported to Babylon, had come under powerful foreign influences. Babylonian culture and religion undoubtedly had a profound impact on those who experienced the exile, even where their response was one of rejection, not of assimilation. It is generally supposed that fresh impetus to Israel's life and worship came from these returned exiles, whereas syncretistic and semi-pagan cults such as those which the pre-exilic prophets had denounced continued to flourish among those who had stayed in the land. On this basis, 57.3-13 and 65.1-5, 11-12 have been understood as describing the debased religion of those left without adequate leadership when the elite of society were deported to Babylon (Bright).

This presupposition no longer goes unquestioned. In a recent essay entitled 'The Origins of the Jewish Diaspora', R.J. Coggins points out what he describes as 'the conspiracy of silence' in the Old Testament regarding the significance of the population who remained in the land. The description in Jeremiah 24 of those who were left in Jerusalem as 'bad figs' and the contemptuous statements in Ezek. 33.23-29 have, in Coggins's view, proved to be remarkably effective propaganda, and he laments the fact that 'much subsequent study, even at the most rigorously academic level, has accepted the claim that the real continuity lay with the exiles'. Yet Ezek. 33.24 indicates that those who remained in the land were not a small number but a large section of the population. The view held by Coggins is not a new one. Noth had already reached a similar conclusion to the effect that 'the tribes left behind in the old country continued to be the centre of Israelite history and Israelite life'.

Chapters 56–66 lack any clear indication of the nature of the dissension, and we must be cautious in assuming that it is to be attributed to a single cause or that the division within the community was along party lines. The complexity of the matter is well illustrated when 66.1-2 is compared with vv. 3 and 5. It is clear that each of these verses originated in a situation of dispute; but, though grouped together editorially, they do not relate to the same situation. To take v. 5 first. Here we have clear evidence of the existence of distinct factions, one of which has gained the upper hand and has taken action to the detriment and exclusion of the other. But the underlying reason for the hostility is not specified. The form of v. 5 suggests that it is a separate oracle not integrally related to the previous verses. Its position here may be due simply to the fact that, like v. 2, it refers to those 'who tremble at his word'. Despite the fact that the opponents are here described as 'brothers', the situation is clearly one of serious tension, although the exact significance of the expression 'cast out' (*niddāh*) is uncertain. It occurs only once elsewhere in the Old Testament (Amos 6.3, where it has a different sense). At this early stage it may not have carried the full technical sense of excommunication which it came to have at a later date when it signified exclusion from the synagogue. The dispute underlying 66.1-2 relates to the question of the nature of God's dwelling among his people, possibly in response to Haggai's insistence on the priority of temple restoration for the community's well-being. It is unlikely, however, to be a total denial of the validity of an earthly sanctuary (on this see above p. 58).

As for v. 3, its relation to v. 1 is unclear and its meaning ambiguous. The Hebrew consists of a series of participial clauses grouped in pairs, but in the absence of connecting words it is uncertain how the two members of each pair, the first referring to legitimate sacrifices, the second to unacceptable actions, are to be related. There are two possible ways of interpreting the meaning: either sacrifice itself in its entirety is being rejected as an appropriate means of worship (for the various possibilities of translation see RSV, NEB) or, more probably, condemnation is directed against those who, while offering the approved forms of sacrifice, also commit the abominations associated with idolatrous cults. In this case the verse is to be understood as a condemnation not of the entire sacrificial system but of syncretistic rites (so Muilenburg, Westermann, Whybray). If this is correct it has no integral connection with vv. 1-2.

The sharp dichotomy exhibited in 65.8-15 suggests, although it does not prove conclusively, that it reflects a worsening of the situation already indicated in 66.5. In contrast to the concerns of 66.1-2 the focus here is on the condemnation of illegitimate cults and, correspondingly, on the central importance of the temple in acceptable worship: to 'forget my holy mountain' is analogous to forsaking the Lord (v. 11). Some persons are accused of involvement in the worship of Gad (Fortune) and Meni (Destiny), cults which flourished in the Hellenistic period and probably earlier. The sharp contrast in the destinies awaiting those described as 'my/his servants' (vv. 8, 9, 13, 14, 15), 'my chosen' (vv. 9, 15), 'my people who have sought me' (v. 10) and, on the other hand, those who have adopted pagan practices (vv. 12-15) sufficiently indicates the bitterness of the divisions which now existed. There is nothing like this rupture within the community anywhere else in the Old Testament (Whybray). To the attempt made by Hanson to trace the causes and progress of this bitter division within the community I shall now turn.

The Nature and Causes of the Dissension

A stimulating and detailed study of the sociological setting of Isaiah 56–66 is to be found in P.D. Hanson's work, *The Dawn of Apocalyptic*, an important and controversial study. The difficulties involved in trying to assign a date to the various literary units within Third Isaiah and the lack of consensus on the subject among scholars have led Hanson, as we have seen already, to adopt a fresh approach which he described as a 'contextual-typological' method. The term 'contextual' refers to the sociological setting of the texts, and 'typological' to the detailed analysis of poetic metre and style which, in conjunction with the genre of the prophetic oracle and its place on the continuum of prophetic and apocalyptic eschatology, is held to give an indication of date on the grounds that 'the development of the canons of poetic composition is analogous to the development of palaeographic style in writing and shape in pottery'. In the matter of distinguishing prophetic eschatology from apocalyptic, Hanson is guided by the criterion that the former is expressed in 'the terms of plain history, real politics, and human instrumentality', whereas the latter arises out of despair of the present age.

Hanson then seeks to elucidate the nature of the opposing factions, and the causes and subsequent development of their mutual hostility. In the eschatological emphasis of these chapters together with the pervading polemical note he finds an indication of their historical setting. The roots of the conflict lay, he believes, in the opposition between two parties, the one eager to maintain the status quo by which they had control of the temple and of the official cult, the other motivated by a sense of rejection resulting from their exclusion from participation in worship, yet lacking the power and resources to wrest control of Zion from their opponents. The former he terms the 'hierocratic party' which consisted of a group of influential priests who had returned from Babylon and seized control of Zion; the latter he describes as visionaries, a group composed of followers of Second Isaiah in association with the disenfranchized Levites who had been excluded by the Zadokites from participation in the service of the temple (cf. Ezek. 44.13). This delineation of the visionary party enables Hanson to explain both the strong resemblances between 56–66 and Second Isaiah, and at the same time to account for the significant differences in emphasis. Third Isaiah, in spite of its strong links with Second Isaiah, is permeated much more deeply by priestly concepts. There is, for example, a recurring emphasis on God's holy mountain, Zion (60.7, 21-22; 61.7; 63.17b-19; 57.13; 65.1-10), for one of the main issues at the heart of the inner-community struggle between visionaries and hierocrats, as Hanson sees it, was concern for the possession of Zion. The association of Levites with the visionaries also explains the emphasis on Moses with its nostalgia for earlier days when Yahweh's relationship to his people was of a more immediate kind without the elaborate structures of kingship and temple (63.11-13).

Hanson regards chs. 60–62 as the restoration programme of the visionaries, and to this same general period he assigns 57.14-19 with its joyful message of comfort and healing for the whole nation. The sudden change of tone in 57.20-21, a passage which according to Hanson's analysis of metre and style is shown to be secondary, is explained as a later attempt, in the light of the developing rift within the community, to modify the initial promise of pardon and salvation which had been addressed to the whole nation. As optimism faded and bitterness grew it was necessary that the promises of Second Isaiah should be reinterpreted if hope was to be sustained in the face of disillusionment and despair. As Hanson puts it, 'disintegrating historical circumstances prompted new modes of conceptualising that restoration hope'. Thus expectations for the future took on a different shape, increasingly detached from the real world of politics and history; and in this way apocalyptic was born.

Hanson regards the rivalry between the two factions as the motivation of chs. 56–66 throughout. Not only is the dissension interpreted consistently as a sectarian struggle, but even the formulation of the restoration programme in 60–62 is to be understood as deliberate opposition to the hierocratic programme in Ezekiel 40–48. For this reason Hanson rejects the widely held view that 63.7–64.12 is an early exilic lament by the community against the external enemies who desecrated the sanctuary when Jerusalem fell in 587, and sees it as further evidence of the bitter hostility between the hierocratic party and the visionaries. It is, he believes, a lament by Levites at their exclusion from the sanctuary by Ezekiel's programme. Thus the enemies who have defiled the sanctuary (63.18) are not external ones but internal rivals. In this context Hanson takes the threefold affirmation, 'you are our Father' (63.16 twice; 64.8), as evidence that this claim by the Levites and their associates has been rejected by the rival faction who claimed the names Abraham and Israel as their own exclusive right (63.16), thus depriving the visionaries of their legitimate part in the covenant community. This circumstance is reflected also, he suggests, in the repeated emphasis on the new names which are bestowed on the faithful (62.4, 12) who have reached the ultimate point of disowning the traditional designation Israel. It is to this new situation that the designation of God as 'father' belongs, a use previously avoided because of unacceptable associations with myth.

One of the main objections to this carefully constructed hypothesis is the unfortunate ambiguity of much of the evidence. Thus in the particular instance discussed here it can equally be argued that Abraham and Israel refer not to the community but to the patriarchs, the human 'fathers' of the nation now unable to assist the present generation in their distress, unlike God who alone 'is a living and present father' (Westermann).

It is to the same situation of sectarian dissension that

Hanson attributes the radical reinterpretation of fasting in 58.1-12, understanding it as an attack on the official cult whose adherents' words are quoted in 58.3a. The polemical tone of the chapter, he argues, is unmistakable. With powerful effect by means of a play on words the inadequacy of their priestly activity is disclosed. The words are replete with irony: in the cult they profess to seek God daily and delight (*ḥāpaṣ*) to know his ways (v. 2a), but to no avail; for it is their own (*ḥēpeṣ*), that they pursue (v. 3). They delight to draw near (*qārab*) to God—a technical term used of the priests' drawing near to God in the Pentateuch and in Ezekiel (Num. 16.40 [17.5]; Ezek. 44.15-16). They have abandoned the 'ordinance' (*mišpāt*) of Yahweh (v. 2b) for the ordinances of the cult.

Similarly in Hanson's view the powerful indictment in 59.1-8 with its vivid images is to be taken not as a word of accusation against the community as a whole but as an attack on those involved in the temple cult. Here the concern, as in 58.3b-4, is with social evils. By their disregard for social obligations the cult is made ineffective: 'Your sins have hidden the Presence' (*pānīm*, v. 2), a technical term of the cult.

Chapter 65, with its separation between the righteous and the wicked which is characteristic of apocalyptic, and also 66.1-16 are seen by Hanson as indicating the widening of the rift. The latter passage is yet another attack on the official cult and on those eager to rebuild the temple—a deliberate rebuttal of Haggai's insistence on the priority of the restoration of the temple. Such restoration, far from demonstrating commitment to the divine will, is an expression of human rebellion against God. In contrast with Haggai's emphasis on the temple, the restoration programme of the visionaries has at its heart a belief in divine intervention and in the miraculous transformation of the community and its land, resulting in universal acknowledgment of God's reign and the establishment of righteousness within a kingdom of priests (61.6).

The bitter vituperation of the visionaries against the hierocratic party reaches its greatest intensity in 56.9–57.13 where once again, according to Hanson's reconstruction of the historical situation, it is no illegitimate cult which is condemned under the imagery of a whore but the official worship centred on the Jerusalem temple. As the social status of the visionaries diminished their other-worldly perspective grew, and their hope for the future was no longer expressed in purely historical terms (59.15-20; 65.17; 66.15-16). According to this view, the 'righteous one' (57.1) who suffers at the hands of wicked leaders is not an individual but the 'righteous servant' of 53.11 with which the visionary group identifies itself. Hanson dates this passage, together with chs. 65 and 66, to the latter part of the sixth century, attributing to the final redactors of the material 56.1-8 and 66.17-24, which he dates to the period 475–425.

The two opposing attitudes which Hanson believes lie at the roots of the conflict in Isaiah 56–66 are apparent not only in this material; they are more widespread in the Old Testament, for not all the biblical literature which comes from the postexilic period reflects the same mainstream orthodoxy. The attitude of the visionaries among whom Isaiah 56–66 originated is reflected also in Zechariah 8–11 and 12–14, and that of the hierocratic party is found not simply in Ezekiel 40–48 with its architectural plans for the restored temple, but also in Haggai, Zechariah 1–8 and the Chronicler. The contrast between Third Isaiah and Ezekiel is seen also in the attitude of the visionaries towards holiness. Whereas Ezekiel regards holiness as restricted to the elite Zadokites who are to take care not to communicate holiness to the people—hence the careful regulation concerning putting off priestly garments (44.19, 23)—for the visionary party it is to be a characteristic of all God's people (60.21; cf. 62.12).

Hanson's case is skilfully argued and cannot be ignored. It is inevitable, however, that his preconceptions and the particular methodology he adopts should have had some influence on the conclusions which he reaches. In his view apocalyptic is a straightforward linear development from prophecy. Since he finds the conditions which produced apocalyptic in the situation reflected in Isaiah 56–66, he is enabled to date the origins of apocalyptic in the sixth to fifth centuries, an earlier period than is generally accepted. An important response to Hanson's thesis concerning the origins and development of apocalyptic has come from R.P. Carroll, and is discussed later in this chapter.

Criticisms of Hanson's Thesis

The importance and stimulus of Hanson's work are widely acknowledged. Nevertheless, there has been considerable criticism of his thesis from several standpoints. One of the main objections to his detailed reconstruction of postexilic Jewish society and to his interpretation of Isaiah 56–66 as arising out of a situation of conflict between the hierocratic and visionary parties is the impossibility of substantiating his argument by any independent historical evidence. There is no doubt that at a later time there were a number of clearly defined parties within Judaism, but there is no other evidence that such existed in the early postexilic period. Another cause for hesitation in accepting his theory is the undeniable fact that some of the key passages on which Hanson bases his argument are capable of a very different interpretation. The lament in 63.7–64.12 is a case in point. As we have seen, Hanson understands this passage as an expression on the part of the Levites, who with the followers of Second Isaiah constituted the visionary group, of their sense of rejection in being excluded from cultic office by the hierocratic group who claimed for themselves the names Abraham and Israel. This view is, however, purely hypothetical, for the use of the name Abraham as a designation for the community is attested nowhere else in the Old Testament. It can more easily be argued that the names refer here to the individual patriarchs, Abraham and Israel, who were regarded as the fathers of the nation, an entirely plausible suggestion in this context where God is called 'Father'. To this we may add that Zimmerli's study of the material has shown nothing in the terminology of the lament to suggest the kind of link with Second Isaiah which Hanson's thesis would require. It is widely accepted that this lament originated in the Palestinian community in the early exilic period as a consequence of devastation by the Babylonian armies.

One of the most cogent objections to Hanson's thesis is the

fact that his definition of the two opposing parties as on the one hand visionary and apocalyptic, represented by Isaiah 56–66, and on the other hand hierocratic, represented by Zechariah 1–8 among others, compels him to deny that any elements of apocalyptic are to be found in the latter, a conclusion the more surprising since it is widely acknowledged that these chapters of Zechariah contain many features which are characteristic of later apocalyptic, among them bizarre visions, interpreting angels, and numerical and animal symbolism. R.J. Coggins takes issue with Hanson on these grounds: his presuppositions have caused him to pay insufficient attention to the eschatological element in both Haggai and Zechariah and, in effect, to force these two prophets into an alien role. Coggins criticizes Hanson, too, for the unwarranted negativity of his attitude towards those books in speaking of 'the ignominious path upon which the prophetic office was set by Haggai and Zechariah'. Hanson's argument, as Coggins points out, leads ultimately to the corollary that a rigid division exists between Zechariah 1–8 and 9–14 since the former chapters represent the hierocratic standpoint while 9–14 undeniably contain apocalyptic elements—a position difficult to sustain in view of the fact that the two sections were eventually brought together into one book. Hanson's argument also obliges him to deny the existence of apocalyptic elements in Ezekiel, since the priestly interests of that book clearly link it with the hierocratic party which, according to Hanson's definition, was diametrically opposed to the visionary party from which apocalyptic sprang. Yet Ezekiel has been called 'the father of apocalyptic' on the grounds that chs. 38–39 form one of the oldest apocalyptic passages in the prophets.

The grave difficulties and uncertainties involved in proceeding from the written text of Isaiah 56–66 to an understanding of the social and political context from which apocalyptic emerged is well illustrated by the very different conclusions to which Williamson comes in his examination of the concept 'Israel' in Third Isaiah. While acknowledging Hanson's approach to the material as 'a most invigorating and creative reading', Williamson discounts the argument that Isaiah 56–66 furnishes evidence of the progressive disruption of the postexilic community to the point at which the visionary party dissociated itself from Israel and disowned the name. Williamson does not subscribe to Hanson's argument that antagonisms within the postexilic community had become polarized to such an extent that all the polemic within Isaiah 56–66 is to be understood in sectarian terms. The fact that both in the prologue (56.8) and in the epilogue (66.20) the name 'Israel' can be used to include the Diaspora as well as the Palestinian community leads Williamson to conclude that there may not have been as much tension existing between the exilic community and those who remained in Palestine as is commonly supposed. 'Though no longer a sovereign state, "Israel" may still have been kept sufficiently alive in the memory and in literature to embrace the communities which had been geographically divided'. In short, Williamson regards chs. 56 and 66 as closer in thought to Zechariah 1–8, where hope is also centred on the restoration of the cult, than to Zechariah 14 which he regards as a later text.

Two other significant references to Israel occur in the lament of 63.7–64.12. Here also Williamson disagrees with Hanson's interpretation of this text and accepts the more commonly held view that it comes from the Palestinian community which remained in the land during the exile. Hanson's argument that Abraham and Israel refer to the community which has rejected the writer and his group is not accepted by Williamson. He takes 'Israel' as a reference to the patriarch on the grounds that the emphasis here on God as father led the writer to make a contrast with the fathers of the nation. There is indeed no evidence for Hanson's view that the returning community ever called itself, or was called, Abraham. Moreover the link between Palestinian Levites and followers of Second Isaiah is, in Williamson's view, improbable in that their attitudes to the return from exile could hardly be expected to coincide.

In short, Williamson concludes that, far from there being evidence in these chapters of two mutually hostile parties, there is no convincing reason for the polemic to be understood in sectarian terms. There is undoubtedly evidence of tension and disagreement, most clearly in 66.5, but the reason for the dissension in this particular instance is uncertain, especially as not a few commentators regard this as an isolated oracle. Westermann indeed, in commenting on the use of the word 'brothers' in this context which speaks so clearly of hostility, notes that although a cleavage is certainly beginning to appear within the community, it has not yet developed to such an extent that one can appropriately speak of 'the parting of the ways between the two groups within the nation'. A further significant argument against Hanson's position is the use in 66.5 (cf. 66.2) of the expression 'you who tremble at his word' to designate the faithful. In that this terminology occurs elsewhere only in Ezra 9.4 and 10.3 with reference to those who are supporters of Ezra we have further evidence, as Williamson points out, that the lines are not yet drawn in party terms.

Some of the most detailed criticism of Hanson's thesis comes from R.P. Carroll. He finds the distinction which Hanson makes between the hierocratic party and the visionaries to be over-rigid—an 'obsessive polarisation'—and his equating of the visionaries with those on the side of the oppressed as over-simplistic. Carroll sounds an appropriate note of warning about taking the anti-cult rhetoric too literally rather than allowing for the exaggeration of polemic. The complete dichotomy which Hanson envisages between prophecy and the cult, represented respectively by the visionaries and the hierocratic party, is detrimental, Carroll argues, in that it conceals from him 'the possibility that apocalyptic may have arisen out of the strong interrelationship between prophecy and cult'. He disagrees, too, with the nature of the distinction which Hanson draws between prophecy and apocalyptic.

Carroll also rightly notes the ambiguity of much of the material and the possibility of interpretations which differ widely from Hanson's. Inevitably the cumulative effect of interpreting the material from different perspectives is to produce widely divergent conclusions. There is circularity, too, Carroll points out, in some of Hanson's arguments. The visionaries, a party opposed to the status quo, support the oppressed. Zechariah, in his support for the rebuilding of the temple, did not align himself with the oppressed (a judgment

Carroll questions with regard to his support of Zerubbabel) but with the official cult; therefore, despite the visionary and eschatological nature of his message, he is not an apocalyptic figure. Thus it is not on the basis of the literary form of Zechariah 1–8, which betrays many of the features of apocalyptic, but on its motivation that Hanson is unwilling to call it apocalyptic. Hanson's arguments lead to a conclusion widely at variance with Gese's view that the earliest example of apocalyptic known to us is the night visions of Zechariah 1–8. In view of Zechariah's priestly associations Gese argues that apocalyptic originated in official circles and not among those cut off from the sources of power.

Apocalyptic Elements in Third Isaiah

Discussion on this subject is beset by the difficulty as to how apocalyptic is to be defined. Hanson, as we have seen, regards Isaiah 56–66 as representing a significant stage in the passage from prophetic to apocalyptic eschatology. The orientation of these chapters is fundamental to Hanson's overall view of the conditions which were responsible for the rise of apocalyptic. This he associates with the sense of powerlessness suffered by the oppressed minority who were excluded by the powerful priestly establishment from active participation in the official cult centred on the Jerusalem temple. In his view it is in respect of these apocalyptic elements that chs. 56–66 differ most markedly from Second Isaiah.

The subject of the rise and development of apocalyptic is a controversial one; and, in contrast to Hanson, some scholars are hesitant to describe any of the material in Third Isaiah as, strictly speaking, apocalyptic, though clearly these chapters already contain elements which occur in a more developed form in the apocalyptic literature of a later period. An example of this latter approach is to be found in Whybray's commentary. Thus he prefers to describe 60.19-20 in more cautious terms as 'showing an apocalyptic tendency'. These verses are in any case, he considers, a later addition in their present context. Here we find a theme common in apocalyptic literature that in the glorious time to come the sun and moon will be replaced by Yahweh as his people's everlasting light (cf. Zech 14.7). Similarly in his comment on 65.17 Whybray warns that it would be 'rash to classify this brief assertion, unique though it is in the OT, as apocalyptic in the full sense. It entirely lacks the detailed description characteristic of the apocalyptic predictions of the end and of the new creation.' He describes it rather as 'the beginning of a new radical theology' which was later developed by the writers of apocalyptic.

The picture of future blessedness found in 65.17-25 is of particular interest in this connection in that it is set within a framework comprising vv. 17 and 25, both of which, in contrast to the intervening verses, are undeniably apocalyptic in tone. The juxtaposition of v. 17 with v. 18 is surprising. In the former there is the promise of new heavens and a new earth. Verse 18, however, immediately narrows the focus: here Yahweh's new creation, far from being cosmic in scope, concerns Jerusalem and the promise of joy for his people. Similarly the transformation of the natural order in 65.25 (cf. 11.6-9) is fundamentally different in character from the preceding promises which are expressed in this-worldly, albeit ideal, terms. This theme again is characteristic of apocalyptic, and Whybray acknowledges the possibility that vv. 17 and 25 have been added with the intention of giving the passage an apocalyptic tone, as may be true also of 66.6 (cf. Westermann). Despite the developed eschatological expectations in 66.18-24, Whybray draws a clear distinction between this passage and what is properly described as apocalyptic. The universal nature of both the judgment and the salvation described here (vv. 23-24), though it differs in character from anything in the rest of Third Isaiah, 'is mainly still far removed from the apocalyptic eschatology' which developed in a later period. The tone of the final verse of the book (66.24) is unique in that it expresses a doctrine of eternal punishment. It has no parallel elsewhere, and Whybray suggests a late date close to the second century BC. It should be noted that all the above passages in which apocalyptic features occur belong to the latter part of Third Isaiah, namely chs. 60–66.

The problem of defining apocalyptic is highlighted in the contrasting attitudes to the divine warrior passage in 63.1-6 found in the commentaries by Whybray and Westermann respectively. Westermann's is a broader definition of apocalyptic, and he includes this passage in addition to the passages referred to above. He asserts categorically, 'the whole thing is apocalyptic'. Here is a portrayal drawn from ancient myth of the divine warrior doing battle against the nations until they are utterly destroyed. The description moves from the specific and historical (Edom and Bozrah) to what is totally beyond history. Westermann compares this passage with the apocalyptic addition of chs. 24–27 which have been inserted into Isaiah 1–39. Whybray, however, excludes it on the grounds that it lacks the cosmic dimensions which are a fundamental characteristic of apocalyptic. In fact he goes so far as to comment that 'the theme of a universal divine victory over the peoples conceived as a single enemy goes little further than such passages in Deutero-Isaiah as 41.8-13'. Although it is chiefly the Babylonians to whom the prophet is there referring, Whybray considers that the fact that no specific name is given 'confers on [these verses] something of a universal character'.

Further Reading

Works other than standard commentaries referred to above:

J. Bright, *A History of Israel* (London: SCM Press, rev. edn, 1972).

R.P. Carroll, 'Twilight of Prophecy or Dawn of Apocalyptic?', *JSOT* 14 (1979), pp. 3-35.

R.J. Coggins, *Haggai, Zechariah and Malachi* (Old Testament Guides; Sheffield: JSOT Press, 1987), p. 59.

—'The Origins of the Jewish Diaspora', in R.E. Clements (ed.), *The World of Ancient Israel* (Cambridge: Cambridge University Press, 1989), esp. p. 166.

H. Gese, 'Anfang und Ende der Apokalyptik dargestellt am Sacharjabuch', *ZTK* (1973), pp. 20-49.

P.D. Hanson, *The Dawn of Apocalyptic* (Philadelphia: Fortress Press, 2nd edn, 1979).

M. Noth, *The History of Israel* (London: A. & C. Black, 1958), p. 291.

H.G.M. Williamson, 'The Concept of Israel in Transition', in Clements (ed.), *Ancient Israel*, esp. pp. 149-52.

Zimmerli, pp. 62-74.

Other works:

P.R. Ackroyd, *Exile and Restoration* (London: SCM Press, 1968).

P.D. Hanson, 'Israelite Religion in the Early Post-exilic Period', in *Ancient Israelite Religion: Essays in Honor of Frank Moore Cross* (ed. P.D. Miller, P.D. Hanson and S.D. McBride; Philadelphia: Fortress Press, 1987).

M.A. Knibb, 'The Emergence of the Jewish Apocalypses', in Coggins, Phillips and Knibb (eds.), *Israel's Prophetic Tradition*.

R. North, 'Prophecy to Apocalyptic via Zechariah', in *Congress Volume, Uppsala 1971* (VTSup, 22; Leiden: Brill, 1972), pp. 47-71.

7

THE SIGNIFICANCE OF
THIRD ISAIAH

Ethical Obligations

SOME OF THE POSTEXILIC prophetic writings give the impression that their concern is more with cultic than with ethical matters. Haggai, for example, attributes the disaster afflicting the nation not to a disregard for the demands of morality but to apathy in setting about the rebuilding of the temple. Malachi's primary concern, too, is with defective worship, with the attitude which diminishes God by the offering of unworthy sacrifices. True, the spiritual motivation of Malachi's message must not be underestimated. It is his aim first and foremost to awaken the community to the sovereignty of God and to their spiritual poverty and the inadequacy of their worship. Yet in spite of this, only minimal attention is paid overtly in that book to those ethical obligations which lie at the heart of all true religion (2.6, 14-16). It is in this respect that the collection of oracles in Isaiah 56–66 is distinctive. There is still a strong concern with acceptable forms of worship and with the central importance of the temple for the community's life, but alongside this there is a deep commitment to ethical matters in the awareness that human relationships form an integral part of relationship to God. This concern with the ethical pervades these chapters. The community's laxity in the area of moral obligation provided for Third Isaiah the reason, at least in part, why the promises of Second Isaiah had remained unfulfilled and why God's

promised intervention in salvation had been delayed (see in
particular 59.1-15a and 63.10–64.12).

Immediately in the opening exhortation of 56.1 we are
aware of this ethical concern. Here eschatology and ethics are
brought into conjunction. The proclamation of the imminence
of salvation is a cause not merely for celebration but for practical action: 'maintain justice, and do what is right' (REB). The
prophet goes on to spell out more specifically the fundamentals
of commitment to Yahweh. Sabbath observance is involved;
but more than this is required, as the following injunction
indicates. The stipulation, 'and keeps his hand from doing any
evil' (v. 2), is not to be interpreted narrowly as if it related only
to religious rituals and institutions. It is the man who does
what is just and right who is blessed, although this prophet is
also well aware that concern with the holy, in effect the
recognition of the transcendence of God, must also have its
place. But it is important to understand correctly the way in
which ethics are related to eschatology in this passage. The
right action (*mišpāt* and *ṣᵉdāqāh*) to which society is summoned is regarded not as the *means* of securing God's saving
intervention, but, on the contrary, as the appropriate preparation of the community which is necessary *because* Yahweh's
deliverance is imminent (for a similar thought see Hos. 12.6).
The terms 'justice' and 'righteousness' are reminiscent of Isa.
5.7 where, in a powerful play on words, Isaiah declares that
God who looks for justice (*mišpāt*) in his people found only
bloodshed (*mišpāḥ*), and in place of righteousness (*ṣᵉdāqāh*)
heard only a cry of distress (*ṣᵉ'āqāh*). It is not uncommon to
find prophets using the literary device of a play on words in
order to heighten the impact of their message, and Isa. 56.1-2
provides one such example, although this is unfortunately not
always apparent in English translations. The word
'righteousness' has two different nuances here. God summons
his people to do 'righteousness' in preparation for the coming
of God's 'righteousness', his action by which he ensures that
right is done, a meaning best conveyed by the translation
'deliverance' (RSV) or 'victory' (REB). It denotes God's intervention to secure the rights of the weak and defenceless
against the rich and powerful.

The distinctive emphasis in Third Isaiah on this strongly ethical note is evident when its opening words (56.1b) are compared with the similar expression in Second Isaiah (46.13) of which they are in all probability a deliberate echo. There the reference to God's intervention in deliverance carries with it no corresponding summons to human action; its purpose is solely to bring comfort to the down-hearted. In Third Isaiah, in contrast, it is a challenge to appropriate action—though this action is not to be regarded as the means of achieving salvation, for this depends not on human effort but solely on Yahweh's action (cf. 59.16; 63.5). Yet the community is not thereby relieved of responsibility. It is in practical action with its social consequences that they are to make preparation for the coming of the promised salvation. (The injunction to 'do righteousness' may perhaps imply that a code of law was already in existence [Whybray]).

Both the style and the content of these opening verses of ch. 56 should be noted. First, there is a deliberate use of repetition. Just as the noun 'righteousness' is repeated in two different senses, so also is the verb 'to keep' in the twofold injunction to 'keep (*šōmēr*) the sabbath' and to 'keep (*šōmēr*) one's hand from all evil'. Secondly, the juxtaposition of the particular and the universal is significant. Sabbath observance is set alongside the avoidance of *all* evil. For this prophet, religious observance and ethical action belong together. Ritual is emptied of its meaning if the obligations of morality are ignored, but at the same time the prophet is aware that social action, if it is to be truly an expression of commitment to God, requires an element of the transcendent, and of this the sabbath served as a reminder. During the exile in Babylon sabbath observance came to be an important external sign of membership of the covenant community. This was not an issue for Second Isaiah, and there is no mention of the sabbath in chs. 40–55. In contrast, the emphasis on sabbath-keeping in Third Isaiah suggests not only that after the exile some had grown slack in this regard (58.13), but that it had become a primary condition for the admission of outsiders into the worshipping community. Nor is it without significance that the sabbath is more than once described as 'holy' (58.13): consequently to infringe it is to

profane it. Its importance is seen from the fact that, whereas
in Malachi blessing was declared to be dependent on the offering of worthy sacrifices, in Third Isaiah it is associated with
observance of the sabbath (56.2, 4-5, 6-7; 58.13-14). In view of
this it is unlikely that the radical reinterpretation of fasting in
terms of social justice in ch. 58 is to be taken as a complete
rejection of the normal rituals of fasting. Rather it constitutes
a powerful plea to preserve the ethical motivation of religious
observance. This matter is discussed more fully below.

The stern denunciation of apathetic, self-centred leadership
with which ch. 56 ends also underlines the moral aspect of
membership of the covenant community, in this instance the
particular responsibilities of leadership. The pursuit of personal gain and self-centred pleasure to the detriment of the
mass of people lays the guilty open to the unmitigated judgment of God. We may note at this point the condemnation of
arrogance (57.15) and the ideal of humility, a note which
reappears in 66.2.

One of the most powerful challenges to moral action is to be
found in ch. 58. With the exception of vv. 1 and 4, this is
framed not in terms of condemnation but of exhortation. The
radical reinterpretation here of the customary practice of
fasting is concerned entirely with matters of social justice, in
particular the exploitation of workers (v. 3) and care for the
deprived and marginalized of society. In noting the number
and variety of words for freedom in v. 6, Westermann comments that 'this is the beginning of that great change which
declared, in God's name, that men and women are of greater
importance than cultic rites directed towards himself'. Not
the ritual motions of fasting, but care for the hungry and
homeless will open the way to the restoration of the people's
own relationship with God and the answering of their prayers
(vv. 4, 9). The thought here is similar to that of Isa. 1.15 which
affirms that the reason for unanswered prayer is that 'your
hands are full of blood'; the remedy is to 'seek justice, correct
oppression'. The literary device of repetition, noted already in
56.1-2, is employed again here, although unfortunately it is
not possible to capture the effect in English: 'if you pour out
yourself ['soul', *nepeš*] for the hungry and satisfy the desire

['soul', *nepeš*] of the afflicted, then shall your light rise in the darkness'. There is no room here for limited, partial concern; whole-hearted commitment to the poor is seen as the prelude to the people's own restoration and that of their devastated cities. It must be said that the implication here that restoration depends on their own prior transformation contrasts with that other strand in some of the earlier prophets where God's gracious initiative in salvation precedes the nation's awareness of its sin and itself leads to repentance (see for example Amos 9.11-15, and most explicitly Ezek. 36.25-31). Nevertheess the strong emphasis on social concern in ch. 58 is in line with the message of the pre-exilic prophets.

The tone of ch. 59 is far sterner than the exhortation of ch. 58, but once again the concern is not with cultic irregularities but with the perversion of justice, particularly in the law courts where injury is done to the innocent (v. 4). Once again the message is categorical; unanswered prayers are not evidence of God's inattentiveness but of human sin. Those who give no justice will look for it in vain themselves (v. 11). Evil has pervaded society both in public and in private relationships (v. 14). The range and variety of Hebrew words for sin in this chapter are impressive. Openly and blatantly, by ignoring the obligations of the covenant, the community dishonours the God whom they profess to worship. It is for this reason that commitment to the covenant, with all that it entailed of moral obligation, was the basis for membership of the body of worshippers for those previously excluded on the grounds of birth or physical defect (56.4-7). Religion and morality cannot be divorced. Relationship to others determines the nature of relationship to God. So it is that, in this context, although probably not in the original form of the oracle, the divine warrior (59.15b-18) takes vengeance not on enemies external to Israel, but on those who, while claiming to belong to the worshipping community, by their actions reject its obligations. Theology and ethics belong together; and this may be the reason why v. 21, which is to some extent at least framed in deuteronomistic terms, has been set in its present context, awkwardly though it stands there (see p. 16): for it is supremely in Deuteronomy that the obligations of the covenant are spelt

out. The instruction of future generations in the word of the
Lord is essential for the community's continuance.

This ethical note pervades the material discussed above. It
appears, too, though in a less pronounced form, in chs. 60–62,
where there is neither accusation nor exhortation but rather
emphasis on the promise of salvation. The meaning of
'righteous' (*ṣaddīqīm*) in 60.21 has been much discussed. Is
this an affirmation that Yahweh's intervention in salvation
includes the transformation of the recipient of that salvation,
or does it mean 'participating in salvation' in a sense similar to
the use of the corresponding noun in 56.1b (Muilenburg)? The
former is more likely since the reference to 'the shoot of my
planting, the work of my hands' recalls the similar metaphor
in Isa. 5.7 (although the Hebrew terms used are not the same)
where also the primary concern is with justice and righteousness. 61.1-3, which comes right at the heart of the central
section of this prophetic material, speaks unequivocally of the
obligation laid on the one commissioned to God's service to
fulfil the requirements of social justice, whether these verses
are understood as descriptive of the prophet's task or applied
to the community as a whole. Equally v. 8 is an unmistakable
affirmation of Yahweh's commitment to justice; it probably
refers here primarily to the freeing of his people from oppression, but it is none the less to be seen as a fundamental aspect of
the nature of God (cf. Ps. 99.4). It is in the light of this that
62.12 is to be understood: 'they shall be called the holy people,
the redeemed of the Lord', for holiness and redemption speak
not only of privilege, of God's action on his people's account,
but of consequent responsibility, of their need for transformation in order to act in accordance with the divine nature.

Is Third Isaiah Materialistic?

The criticism is sometimes made that the eschatological
expectations of Third Isaiah are more worldly and material-
istic in character than those of Second Isaiah. It is true that
the era of salvation is depicted in chs. 60–62 in terms of
material prosperity and of the physical enrichment of temple
and city. To see this in its true perspective, however, we must

set it in the context of history. For underlying this is the motif of reversal, the transforming action of God who, in the promised era of salvation, will rescue the helpless, restore the ruined temple and devastated cities, and return possessions looted and pillaged by strangers. It is easy to be misled by the material nature of the images which are used into thinking that this is an expression of a rather gross materialism. But

> the passionate hunger of the prophet is not for wealth, or a beautiful city, or to have kings as his servants, but for God and God's redemption... The disparagement of Old Testament eschatology as materialistic in contrast to the spirituality of New Testament eschatology is unjustified and fails to grasp the true intention of the prophet (Smart).

Certainly the portrayal of salvation in material terms is not the whole picture. It is balanced by the expression of restored communion between Israel and God in terms of the hearing and answering of prayer. Westermann sees this aspect of Third Isaiah's message as of particular importance for the meaning of salvation (58.9a; 65.24; cf. 30.10). 'Being saved', he says, 'consists in the interrelation of word and answer. Salvation is not described as a state of bliss, but as the constancy of the dialogical relationship between man and God'. We may add that it is in keeping with this that the temple is designated 'a house of prayer for all peoples' (56.7).

Universality and Particularity

The significance of the temple for all nations brings us to another important theme in Isaiah 56–66, which is evident particularly in its framework. Here in the final canonical form of the material we find a radical departure from the restrictive regulations found in certain other parts of the Old Testament. In the light of the exile this change is particularly significant; it is a reaction not, as might have been expected, of bitterness and hostility to non-Jews but of generous welcome into the worshipping community. There is an unequivocal note of universalism in the concluding verses of ch. 66: both God's judgment and his presence apply to 'all flesh', Jew and Gentile alike (66.16, 23-24). None is spared the solemn possibility of judgment, but neither is anyone who makes a response excluded from the divine presence. The most remarkable statements of all occur in 66.18-21. Here God is envisaged as gathering 'all nations and tongues' that they may witness his glory. But this is not all. Verse 19 is still more remarkable. As the text stands, despite some ambiguities, it conveys the idea of mission, the proclamation of God's greatness in distant lands. The list of nations may be compared with the similar list in 11.11, but there, in contrast, the concern is solely with bringing scattered Israelites to their homeland, a not unfamiliar theme. The contribution of Third Isaiah in this significant area must not be minimized even if one accepts Westermann's argument that this remarkable conception of mission has been toned down by the addition of vv. 20 and 22-24. Despite Westermann's dismissal of these verses as 'conservative and absolutely static', and opposed to the idea of mission, it should not go unnoticed that even in v. 20 the nations, who are to be the means of bringing scattered Israel home, are described as 'a clean vessel'. Still more radical is the statement in v. 21 which allows for some of these to be priests and Levites. Second Isaiah affirms that the mission of the servant is to reach beyond the confines of Israel to be 'a light to the nations' (49.6), but the vision which is given expression in 66.21 goes beyond even this in its acceptance that some who are not by birth members of the community may be admitted to the service of the sanctuary. This is a far cry from the prescription in Num. 18.1-7 which imposes the death penalty on any not of Aaronic or Levitical descent who presume to serve within the sanctuary (cf. Ezek. 44.7-9, 15). With 66.21 we have moved far beyond the central core of Third Isaiah where the nations simply serve the purpose of restoring Israel to its homeland (60.10, 12-14; 61.5-6). Ritual law here, as also in 56.3-7, is abrogated by the prophetic word. With the importance thus attached to the word given through the prophet may be linked those passages which emphasize reverence for the divine word as the mark of the faithful within the community (66.2, 5).

The chief significance of this radical attitude towards admission to the people of God lies in its implications for the nature of the covenant community. It is no longer birth which is the passport to membership of the community but the voluntary undertaking of allegiance to Yahweh. There is consequently a severance between the religious community and the state (Westermann). This is in marked contrast to the restrictive attitude of Neh. 9.2 with its exclusion of all foreigners (*bᵉnē nēkār*, the same expression as in 56.3, 6). Yet alongside this element of the universal in these chapters there is another strand which is in tension with it and which is never obliterated, but appears as strongly in the framework as it does elsewhere. This is the particularity of the emphasis on Jerusalem which pervades every part of the material. The promise of salvation in chs. 60–62 is focused on Jerusalem. It is this city which is addressed in the feminine imperatives of 60.1; and the commission given in 61.2 to 'comfort all that mourn' is immediately qualified as 'those who mourn in Zion'. Yet even here there is perhaps a hint of the universal. After the song of praise on Jerusalem's account, 'robed in deliverance, arrayed in victory' (REB; 61.10) the concluding verse of the chapter envisages God making 'his victory and renown blossom before all the nations'. It is possible to argue that the nations here are merely witnesses of God's saving action. On the basis of a pattern in the Psalms, however, where the nations are summoned to join in praise of the universal king, it may be correct to detect a universal note here also. The victory ('righteousness', *ṣᵉdāqāh*) celebrated in 61.11 need not be understood in terms of conquest of the nations (contrast 60.12, generally agreed to be a secondary insertion) but of Yahweh's ensuring that right is done in the all-too-often oppressive world.

Democratization

The process of 'democratization' of Israel's sacral institutions, which begins with Second Isaiah in 55.3-5, is taken further in Third Isaiah. One of the notable passages in this connection is 62.3, where Israel in the time of salvation is to be 'a crown of beauty in the hand of the Lord, and a royal diadem in the hand of your God'. A similar democratization may perhaps be evident in 61.1-3, although the interpretation of this passage is open to debate. It is generally understood as a reference to the prophetic figure with whom the nucleus of the oracles in 60–62 may be thought to have originated (see above pp. 75-76). Hanson, however, disagrees with the view that 61.1-3 refers to the prophet's call. Instead he regards these themes, which are taken from the Servant Songs of Second Isaiah, as applied in the postexilic period to the community as a whole. A comparable democratization of a traditional office appears also, he believes, in 61.6 where the members of the community are themselves to be known as 'priests of the Lord'. In this amalgamation within ch. 61 of the priestly with the prophetic office he sees a reminiscence of Moses' role.

Conclusion

For Westermann the importance of Third Isaiah lies primarily in the fact that through these oracles the tradition of pre-exilic and exilic prophecy was preserved as a still valid word of God. In the spiritual vacuum created by the non-fulfilment of the glowing promises of Second Isaiah this later prophet succeeded in keeping faith alive, confident that God would yet intervene in salvation. It is difficult, Westermann writes, for the modern reader to appreciate fully what it meant in that situation of despair to hold on to God's promises: 'the fact that Trito-Isaiah's proclamation does this is what gives it its categorical importance in the history of prophecy'.

Yet to restrict the significance of chs. 56–66 to the preservation and reapplication of an earlier prophetic message is to undervalue their contribution to the shaping of Israelite thought. There are two areas in which the message of Third Isaiah is of a radical kind, entailing transformation both of the nature of the worshipping community and of the essence of acceptable religious observance. These chapters affirm that the heart of true religion consists in putting into practice in daily living Yahweh's own commitment to social justice (cf. Mic. 6.8). It is no longer to be the privilege of birth and physical descent that ensures a place within the covenant community, but personal commitment in active obedience to God.

Although the historical circumstances and content of Third Isaiah's message differ widely from those of the eighth-century Amos, the radical challenge of the message is the same. On the one hand, to be of Israel is not a guarantee of salvation, for all stand under judgment (cf. Amos 5.18); on the other hand, people of foreign descent are not excluded from relationship with the saving Lord. Throughout these chapters there is an emphasis on practical action as a means of transforming both society and the worshipping community. The needs of individuals, eunuchs returned from royal service in exile, foreigners, the poor and oppressed, all these are taken into account. It is not surprising that the commission given in 61.1-3 is taken in the New Testament as a fit description of the ministry of Jesus of Nazareth (Lk. 4.18-19).

The task of a prophet is to bring the word of God to bear on a specific situation and to address the needs of his contemporaries. With this as the touchstone the authenticity of the oracles contained in Isaiah 56–66 is confirmed. There are words of comfort and assurance in a difficult and depressing situation, but always words of challenge to renewal, turning the hearers away from concentration on their own problems, and reminding them of the greatness of the God whom they profess to worship. In a manner not unworthy of earlier prophets these chapters affirm that social obligation is a part of relationship to God, a part of worship. This is no message to lull the hearers into complacency, allowing them to hide from the stern realities of the time. It is the word of those who truly stand in Israel's great prophetic tradition.

Further Reading

W.A.M. Beuken, 'The Main Theme of Trito-Isaiah "The Servants of Yahweh" ', *JSOT* 47 (1990), pp. 81-85.

W. Brueggemann, 'Unity and Dynamic in the Isaiah Tradition', *JSOT* 29 (1984), pp. 99-102.

C.R. Seitz, 'The Theological Legacy of a Struggling Community', in Seitz (ed.), *Reading and Preaching the Book of Isaiah*.

INDEXES

INDEX OF BIBLICAL REFERENCES

INDEX OF AUTHORS